Contracts Under the Scalpel: Case Dissections

Common Law Contracts

(Law in Pieces)

Anjanette G. Seymour, LL.M., LL.B. (Hons.)

This work is published as part of the *Law in Pieces* series of study snippets. It is intended as an educational aid and should not be construed as a full textbook or novel. Nothing in this volume constitutes legal advice, nor does it create an attorney–client relationship. Readers should consult authoritative sources, case law, and qualified legal instructors for comprehensive guidance.

This book explains judicial opinions and legal doctrine in clear, original language. All case names and quotations from judicial opinions are in the public domain. The anatomical framework, narrative explanations, summaries, diagrams, and pedagogical structure are original works created by the author. Any errors or interpretations are the author's own.

Cover Design: Anjanette G. Seymour

ISBN: 9798995892342

TABLE OF CONTENTS

DEDICATION

For every student who has ever felt behind, unseen, or unsure — you belong here. You are capable. You are enough.

And for the ones who taught me that clarity is an act of love: this book is for you.

EPIGRAPH

"Clarity is the kindest form of strength."

— Anjanette G. Seymour

PREFACE

This book is part of the *Law in Pieces* series — a project rooted in the belief that legal education should be accessible, intuitive, and emotionally resonant. So I began writing the books I wish I had as a student: books that speak plainly, teach deeply, and honor the humanity behind every dispute.

Contracts Under the Scalpel is the culmination of that vision. It is the product of countless hours of reading, writing, refining, and reimagining what legal education can be. It is also the product of resilience — of choosing to build something meaningful even when life demanded detours, reinventions, and new beginnings.

If this book helps even one student feel seen, capable, and empowered, then every page has done its work.

Thank you for choosing to learn with me.

INTRODUCTION

Law students often enter contracts feeling as though they've stepped into a foreign country — one where the language is familiar, but the meanings are elusive. Cases blur together, doctrines feel abstract, and the heart of the subject hides beneath layers of terminology and tradition.

Contracts Under the Scalpel was born from a simple conviction: students deserve clarity, warmth, and a sense of belonging in the law.

This book dissects the core doctrines of contract law through the cases that built them. But instead of presenting those cases as cold artifacts, each one is opened with care — anatomically, narratively, and pedagogically — so students can see the living structure beneath the surface.

Every chapter follows the same rhythm:

- Pulse — the human tension beating beneath the dispute
- Veins — the flow of communication and reliance
- Muscle — the doctrinal strength of the agreement
- Heart — the core question the court must resolve
- Spine — the rule that holds the case upright
- Brain — the court's reasoning
- Lungs — how the doctrine expands or contracts
- Stomach — the digestible takeaway

- Skin — the holding
- Fractures — the cracks, tensions, and doctrinal shifts, where the law is still evolving.

This structure is designed to help students not only *understand* the law but *feel* it — to see doctrine as something alive, purposeful, and deeply human.

My hope is that this book becomes a companion: a guide through confusion, a source of epiphany, and a reminder that the law is not a fortress but a landscape — one you can navigate with confidence and grace.

Part I. Foundations and Agreement

1. Offer & Acceptance

Case 1 — *Carlill v. Carbolic Smoke Ball Co. (1893)*

Pulse — What intention beats beneath the surface?

At the heart of this case is a company trying to sell a miracle cure during an influenza epidemic. Their advertisement wasn't just marketing — it carried a heartbeat of assurance, a promise meant to inspire trust. They said:

Use our smoke ball as directed, and if you still get the flu, we'll pay you £100.

They even claimed to have deposited £1,000 in the bank to show their sincerity.

The Pulse here is intention — did the company intend this promise to be taken seriously, or was it mere puffery?

Mrs. Carlill believed it. She relied on it. And she got sick anyway.

Veins — How does offer and acceptance flow?

This case is the bloodstream of unilateral contracts.

- The offer flowed outward to the world through the advertisement.
- The acceptance flowed back silently when Mrs. Carlill used the smoke ball as instructed.
- No notice of acceptance was required — the act itself completed the contract.

The Veins show us that performance can be acceptance when the offeror invites it.

Muscle — What gives this agreement enforceable strength?

The Muscle is built from:

- Consideration: Mrs. Carlill used the product, endured inconvenience, and increased sales for the company.
- Reliance: She trusted the promise and acted on it.
- Certainty: The terms were clear — use the smoke ball three times daily for two weeks.

The contract wasn't fragile. It had structure, weight, and enforceability.

Heart — What is the core dispute?

The company refused to pay the £100, arguing:

- The ad wasn't a real offer
- It was "mere puff"
- No contract existed
- Mrs. Carlill didn't notify them of acceptance
- The terms were too vague
- It was impossible to contract with "the whole world"

The Heart is simple: Was the advertisement a binding offer capable of acceptance?

Spine — What rule holds this case upright?

The court articulated the backbone of unilateral contracts:

- An advertisement can be an offer if it shows clear intention to be bound.
- Performance of the conditions is acceptance.
- No notification of acceptance is required when the offeror waives it by the nature of the offer.
- Consideration exists when the offeree performs the requested act.

This Spine supports nearly every modern doctrine of unilateral contracts.

Brain — How does the court reason through this?

The court's reasoning is calm, logical, and deeply human:

1. The deposit of £1,000 showed sincerity, not puffery.
2. The ad was specific, not vague.
3. The company invited performance, not communication.
4. Mrs. Carlill did exactly what the ad required.
5. The law must protect people who rely on clear promises.

The Brain of this case teaches students that courts look at substance over form, and at intention over clever argument.

Lungs — How does this doctrine expand or contract?

This case expands contract law by:

- Recognizing unilateral offers to the public
- Allowing acceptance through performance

- Protecting consumers from deceptive promises
- Emphasizing intention and reliance

It contracts the idea that advertisements are always invitations to treat.

Stomach — The digestible takeaway

If a company makes a clear promise to the world, invites performance, and signals seriousness, then:

- That promise can be an offer
- Performance is acceptance
- A contract is formed
- The promise must be honored

Students walk away thinking: *"Oh — this is how unilateral contracts actually work."*

Skin — The holding

The court held that:

- The advertisement was a valid offer
- Mrs. Carlill accepted by performing the conditions
- Consideration existed
- A binding contract was formed
- The company owed her £100

Fractures — Cracks, tensions, and doctrinal shifts

- Some argue the court stretched intention to protect consumers.
- Others say the case blurs the line between offers and invitations to treat.
- It raises questions about how far unilateral offers can extend.
- It foreshadows modern consumer protection law.

But the fractures don't weaken the case — they make it richer.

Case 2 — *Pharmaceutical Society v. Boots Cash Chemists* (1953)

Pulse — What intention beats beneath the surface?

Boots wasn't trying to trick anyone. They were simply modernizing: moving from behind-the-counter sales to **self-service shopping**, a revolutionary idea at the time. But the Pharmaceutical Society worried that this new system allowed customers to "buy" regulated medicines without a pharmacist's supervision.

The Pulse here is **intention in the retail environment**:

- Did Boots intend the shelf display to be an **offer**?
- Or merely an **invitation** for customers to bring items to the cashier?

This case beats with the question: **When does a sale actually happen?**

Veins — How does offer and acceptance flow?

This case teaches students the **circulation of contract formation in everyday life**:

- The **shelf display** is *not* an offer.
- The **customer picking up the item** is *not* acceptance.
- The **customer presenting the item at the cashier** is the **offer**.
- The **cashier's approval** is the **acceptance**.

The Veins show that **the flow of offer and acceptance happens**

at the checkout, not the shelf.

This is the bloodstream of modern retail.

Muscle — What gives this agreement enforceable strength?

The Muscle comes from:

- **Control**: Boots retains the right to refuse the sale at the cashier.
- **Supervision**: A pharmacist is stationed at the counter to approve regulated items.
- **Structure**: The transaction is not complete until the cashier accepts the customer's offer.

The enforceability is strong because the system preserves **professional oversight** and **legal compliance**.

Heart — What is the core dispute?

The Pharmaceutical Society argued:

- The sale occurred **when the customer picked up the item,**
- meaning regulated medicines were being "sold" without pharmacist supervision.

Boots argued:

- The sale occurred **at the cashier,**
- where a pharmacist was present.

The Heart is the question: **When does a sale legally occur in a self-service store?**

Spine — What rule holds this case upright?

The court reaffirmed a foundational rule:

A display of goods is an invitation to treat, not an offer.

This means:

- The customer makes the offer at the cashier.
- The store accepts (or rejects) the offer at that moment.
- The sale is not complete until acceptance.

This Spine supports nearly every modern retail transaction.

Brain — How does the court reason through this?

The court's reasoning is calm, practical, and grounded in commercial reality:

1. **Self-service does not change the legal structure of sales.**
2. The store must retain the right to refuse a sale — shelves cannot bind them.
3. The pharmacist's presence at the cashier ensures compliance with regulations.
4. The customer's act of picking up an item is **not** acceptance — it is merely selection.

The Brain teaches students that **law adapts to commerce**, not the other way around.

Lungs — How does this doctrine expand or contract?

This case expands contract law by:

- Recognizing self-service shopping as compatible with traditional doctrine
- Clarifying the legal moment of sale
- Protecting retailers from unintended contractual obligations
- Reinforcing consumer protection through controlled acceptance

It contracts the idea that **any display of goods can be an offer**.

Stomach — The digestible takeaway

Students should walk away knowing:

- Shelves invite you to make an offer.
- You make the offer at the cashier.
- The store accepts or rejects your offer there.
- The sale is not complete until acceptance.

This is the backbone of everyday shopping.

Skin — The holding

The court held that:

- The shelf display was an **invitation to treat**
- The customer's presentation of the item was the **offer**
- The cashier's approval was the **acceptance**
- Boots complied with the law because a pharmacist supervised the acceptance stage

Fractures — Cracks, tensions, and doctrinal shifts.

- Some argue the doctrine is artificial in a world of barcodes and self-checkout.
- Others say it protects retailers from being bound by shelf errors.
- It raises questions about online shopping, where the "offer" and "acceptance" moments shift again.
- It foreshadows the evolution of contract formation in modern commerce.

The fractures make the case feel alive — not outdated.

Case 3 — *Fisher v. Bell (1961)*

Pulse — What intention beats beneath the surface?

This case begins with something deceptively simple: a shopkeeper places a **flick knife** in his window with a price tag.

No drama. No negotiation. Just a display.

But beneath that quiet surface beats a question of **intention**:

- Did the shopkeeper intend to **offer** the knife for sale?
- Or was he merely **inviting** customers to come inside and begin the process?

The Pulse here is the tension between **appearance** and **legal intention**.

Veins — How does offer and acceptance flow?

Students often assume:

"If it has a price tag, it must be an offer."

This case gently corrects that instinct.

The Veins show the true flow:

- The **shop window display** is *not* an offer.
- The **customer entering the shop** is not acceptance.
- The **customer expressing interest** is the **offer**.
- The **shopkeeper agreeing to sell** is the **acceptance**.

The bloodstream of contract formation remains consistent with *Boots.*

Muscle — What gives this agreement enforceable strength?

The Muscle here is subtle:

- **Control**: The shopkeeper must retain the right to refuse a sale.
- **Legal compliance**: Selling certain weapons is regulated.
- **Structure**: A display cannot bind a seller to a contract they never intended to make.

The enforceability of any agreement depends on **mutual intention**, not mere display.

Heart — What is the core dispute?

The police charged the shopkeeper with "offering" a flick knife for sale, which was illegal.

The Heart of the case is the question:

Does displaying a knife with a price tag amount to "offering it for sale"?

If yes → he committed an offense. If no → he did nothing wrong.

Spine — What rule holds this case upright?

The court reaffirmed a foundational rule:

A display of goods — even with a price tag — is an invitation to treat, not an offer.

This Spine is the backbone of retail law.

Brain — How does the court reason through this?

The court's reasoning is crisp and doctrinal:

1. **Contract law principles apply** even in criminal contexts.
2. A display is an **invitation**, not an offer.
3. The seller must retain the right to refuse a sale.
4. The actual "offer" occurs when the customer proposes to buy.
5. The shopkeeper "accepts" by agreeing to sell.

The Brain teaches students that **legal meaning is not the same as everyday meaning**.

Lungs — How does this doctrine expand or contract?

This case expands the clarity of the invitation-to-treat doctrine:

- Shop windows
- Price tags
- Catalogues
- Online listings
- Advertisements

All fall under the same principle.

It contracts the idea that **any display with a price is an offer**.

Stomach — The digestible takeaway

Students should walk away knowing:

- A shop window display is **not** an offer.
- Even with a price tag, it is an **invitation to treat**.
- The customer makes the **offer**.
- The shopkeeper **accepts** or rejects.
- This protects sellers from unintended legal obligations.

This case is the quiet guardian of modern commerce.

Skin — The holding

The court held that:

- The display of the flick knife was an **invitation to treat**, not an offer.
- Therefore, the shopkeeper **did not commit the offense** of "offering" the knife for sale.

Fractures — Cracks, tensions, and doctrinal shifts

- Critics argue the decision is overly formalistic.
- It highlights the gap between **legal language** and **ordinary language**.
- It raises questions about consumer expectations in modern retail.
- It foreshadows debates about online shopping, where "Add to Cart" complicates the offer/acceptance sequence.

The fractures make the doctrine richer, not weaker.

Case 4 — *Partridge v. Crittenden (1968)*

Pulse — What intention beats beneath the surface?

This case begins with a simple newspaper advertisement:

"Bramblefinch cocks and hens, 25 shillings each."

No drama. No bargaining. Just a man listing birds for sale.

But beneath that quiet ad beats a question of **intention**:

- Did Partridge intend to **offer** the birds for sale?
- Or was he merely **inviting** interested buyers to contact him?

The Pulse here is the difference between **advertising** and **committing** — a distinction that protects sellers from accidental legal liability.

Veins — How does offer and acceptance flow?

This case continues the bloodstream of contract formation that students began to see in *Boots* and *Fisher v. Bell*:

- The **advertisement** is *not* an offer.
- The **interested buyer's response** is the **offer**.
- The **seller's acceptance** completes the contract.

The Veins show that **advertisements circulate invitations**, not binding promises.

Muscle — What gives this agreement enforceable strength?

The Muscle here is built from:

- **Control**: Advertisers must retain the right to choose whom to sell to.
- **Practicality**: If ads were offers, sellers could be forced into contracts with unlimited buyers.
- **Legal protection**: Criminal liability should not arise from mere advertisements.

The enforceability of any agreement depends on **mutual assent**, not unilateral publication.

Heart — What is the core dispute?

Partridge was charged with "offering" a protected wild bird for sale — an offense under the Protection of Birds Act.

The Heart of the case is the question:

Does placing an advertisement amount to "offering" the item for sale?

If yes → Partridge committed a crime. If no → he did nothing wrong.

Spine — What rule holds this case upright?

The court reaffirmed a foundational rule:

Advertisements are invitations to treat, not offers.

This Spine protects sellers from being bound by every response to an ad.

Brain — How does the court reason through this?

The court's reasoning is practical and grounded in commercial reality:

1. **Advertisements are invitations**, not offers.
2. If ads were offers, sellers could be forced into unlimited contracts.
3. The advertiser must retain the right to accept or reject buyers.
4. Criminal statutes should not be interpreted to impose liability where intention is absent.
5. The buyer's response is the **offer**, not the ad itself.

The Brain teaches students that **contract law protects fairness and practicality**, not rigid literalism.

Lungs — How does this doctrine expand or contract?

This case expands the clarity of the invitation-to-treat doctrine:

- Newspaper ads
- Online listings
- Classifieds
- Flyers
- Social media posts
- Marketplace listings

All fall under the same principle.

It contracts the idea that **any advertisement can be an offer**.

Stomach — The digestible takeaway

Students should walk away knowing:

- Advertisements are **not** offers.
- They are **invitations to treat**.
- The buyer makes the **offer**.
- The seller chooses whether to **accept**.
- This protects sellers from unintended legal obligations.

This case is the quiet guardian of modern advertising.

Skin — The holding

The court held that:

- The advertisement was an **invitation to treat**, not an offer.
- Therefore, Partridge **did not commit the offense** of "offering" the bird for sale.

Fractures — Cracks, tensions, and doctrinal shifts

- Critics argue the doctrine can feel artificial in the age of online shopping.
- It highlights the gap between **legal meaning** and **everyday meaning**.
- It raises questions about automated sales systems.
- It foreshadows modern debates about online "Buy Now" buttons.

The fractures make the doctrine more nuanced, not weaker.

Case 5 — *Harvey v. Facey (1893)*

Pulse — What intention beats beneath the surface?

This case begins with a telegram — quick, clipped, and deceptively simple.

Harvey wanted to buy a property called **Bumper Hall Pen**. He sent a message asking:

"Will you sell us Bumper Hall Pen? Telegraph lowest cash price."

Facey replied:

"Lowest price for Bumper Hall Pen £900."

Harvey immediately responded:

"We agree to buy for £900."

But beneath these short messages beats a deeper question of **intention**:

- Did Facey intend to **offer** the property for sale?
- Or was he merely **providing information**?

The Pulse here is the difference between **interest** and **commitment**.

Veins — How does offer and acceptance flow?

Students often assume:

"If someone gives a price, that must be an offer."

This case gently corrects that instinct.

The Veins show the true flow:

- Harvey's first telegram was a **request for information**, not an offer.
- Facey's reply was **information**, not an offer.
- Harvey's "We agree to buy" was an **offer**, not an acceptance.
- Facey never accepted.

The bloodstream of contract formation never completed the circuit.

Muscle — What gives this agreement enforceable strength?

The Muscle is missing — and that's the point.

For a contract to have enforceable strength, it needs:

- **Clear intention**
- **Definite terms**
- **Mutual assent**

Here, Facey never expressed an intention to sell. He only stated the **lowest price he would consider**.

Information alone has no contractual muscle.

Heart — What is the core dispute?

Harvey claimed that Facey's reply ("Lowest price £900") was an **offer**, and that his own telegram ("We agree to buy") was **acceptance**, forming a binding contract.

The Heart of the case is the question:

Does stating a minimum price amount to an offer to sell?

If yes → Facey is bound. If no → no contract exists.

Spine — What rule holds this case upright?

The court reaffirmed a foundational rule:

****A statement of price is not an offer.**

It is merely information.**

This Spine is essential for distinguishing between:

- Negotiation
- Inquiry
- Information
- Actual offers

Brain — How does the court reason through this?

The court's reasoning is precise and elegant:

1. Harvey's first telegram was a **request for information**, not an offer.
2. Facey's reply was **information**, not an intention to sell.
3. A valid offer requires **clear intention to be bound**.
4. Facey never said "I will sell."
5. Harvey's "We agree to buy" was an **offer**, not acceptance.
6. Without acceptance, there is **no contract**.

The Brain teaches students that **clarity of intention is the**

lifeblood of contract formation.

Lungs — How does this doctrine expand or contract?

This case expands contract law by:

- Clarifying the difference between **information** and **offers**
- Protecting parties from being bound by casual statements
- Reinforcing the need for **clear intention** in contract formation

It contracts the idea that **any mention of price can be an offer**.

Stomach — The digestible takeaway

Students should walk away knowing:

- Asking for a price is **not** an offer.
- Giving a price is **not** an offer.
- A contract requires **intention**, not just information.
- Harvey's "We agree to buy" was an offer — but it was never accepted.

This case teaches the quiet discipline of contract formation.

Skin — The holding

The court held that:

- Facey's telegram was **not an offer**, only information.
- Harvey's reply was an **offer**, not acceptance.
- No contract was formed.

Fractures — Cracks, tensions, and doctrinal shifts.

Case 6 — *Gibson v. Manchester City Council (1979)*

Pulse — What intention beats beneath the surface?

This case begins with a man, Mr. Gibson, who wanted to buy his council house — something many families dreamed of during that era. He received a letter from the City Council stating:

"The Corporation **may be prepared to sell** the house to you for £2,180."

Those words — "may be prepared to sell" — carry a soft, hesitant heartbeat. Not a promise. Not a commitment. Just a possibility.

The Pulse here is the delicate distinction between **interest** and **intention**.

Veins — How does offer and acceptance flow?

Students often assume:

"If someone gives a price, that must be an offer."

But the Veins of this case show a more careful circulation:

- The Council's letter was **not** an offer — it was an invitation to negotiate.
- Gibson's application form was **not** acceptance — it was an **offer**.
- The Council never accepted his offer because the political administration changed.

The bloodstream of contract formation never completed the loop.

Muscle — What gives this agreement enforceable strength?

The Muscle is missing here — and that absence is the lesson.

For a contract to have enforceable strength, it needs:

- **Clear intention to be bound**
- **Definite terms**
- **Mutual assent**

The Council's letter lacked the first element. It was cautious, conditional, and incomplete.

Without intention, there is no muscle.

Heart — What is the core dispute?

Gibson argued that the Council's letter was an **offer**, and that his application form was **acceptance**, forming a binding contract to sell him the house.

The Heart of the case is the question:

Does "may be prepared to sell" amount to an offer?

If yes → the Council must sell the house. If no → no contract exists.

Spine — What rule holds this case upright?

The court reaffirmed a foundational rule:

****A statement of willingness to negotiate is not an offer.**

Clear intention is required.**

This Spine protects parties from being bound by tentative or exploratory language.

Brain — How does the court reason through this?

The court's reasoning is precise and deeply rooted in the logic of contract formation:

1. The Council's letter was **not an offer** — it was an invitation to treat.
2. The phrase "may be prepared to sell" shows **no commitment.**
3. The letter invited Gibson to **apply**, not to accept.
4. Gibson's application was an **offer**, not acceptance.
5. The Council never accepted his offer.
6. Without acceptance, there is **no contract**.

The Brain teaches students that **language matters**, and courts read intention carefully.

Lungs — How does this doctrine expand or contract?

This case expands contract law by:

- Clarifying the importance of **precise wording**
- Reinforcing the need for **clear intention**
- Protecting public bodies from unintended contractual obligations
- Teaching students to distinguish between **offers** and **preliminary negotiations**

It contracts the idea that **any communication with a price can**

be an offer.

Stomach — The digestible takeaway

Students should walk away knowing:

- "May be prepared to sell" is **not** an offer.
- It is an **invitation to treat**.
- A contract requires **clear intention**, not hopeful interpretation.
- Gibson's application was an offer — but it was never accepted.

This case teaches the discipline of reading language with legal precision.

Skin — The holding

The House of Lords held that:

- The Council's letter was **not an offer**.
- Gibson's application was an **offer**, not acceptance.
- The Council never accepted.
- Therefore, **no contract was formed**.

Fractures — Cracks, tensions, and doctrinal shifts

- Critics argue the decision is overly formalistic.
- It highlights the tension between **fairness** and **doctrinal clarity**.

- It raises questions about public policy and administrative change.
- It foreshadows modern debates about government promises and reliance.

The fractures make the case feel human — because real people's hopes were involved.

Case 7 — *Storer v. Manchester City Council (1974)*

Pulse — When does intention crystallize into commitment?

This case begins with another hopeful council-house tenant, Mr. Storer. But unlike Gibson, the heartbeat here is strong, steady, and unmistakably contractual.

The Council sent him a letter that didn't whisper possibility. It spoke in the language of completion:

"If you will sign the agreement and return it to me, I will send you the agreement signed on behalf of the council."

This is not the soft pulse of "may be prepared." This is the firmer rhythm of "do this, and we will do that."

The Pulse here is the moment where intention becomes action, and action becomes agreement.

Veins — How does offer and acceptance flow?

The circulation in this case is clean and direct:

- The Council's letter was an offer.
- The enclosed "Agreement for Sale" contained complete, definite terms.
- Storer accepted by signing and returning the agreement.
- The Council's later political shift did not interrupt the flow — because the contract had already formed.

Where Gibson's veins never completed the loop, Storer's flow is uninterrupted and contractually alive.

Muscle — What gives this agreement enforceable strength?

The Muscle here is robust because all three pillars of formation are present:

- Clear intention to be bound The Council's letter was not exploratory — it was directive.
- Definite terms Price, property, and conditions were all settled.
- Mutual assent Storer did exactly what the Council asked to finalize the deal.

The Muscle is the Council's own language: "If you sign, we will sign." That is the anatomy of commitment.

Heart — What is the core dispute?

Storer argued:

- The Council made an offer.
- He accepted it by signing and returning the agreement.
- A binding contract existed.

The Council argued:

- No contract existed because they had not yet countersigned.
- A new administration had changed policy.

The Heart of the case is the question:

Does a contract form when one party completes the required act of acceptance, even if the other party has not yet performed the administrative step of signing?

The court said yes.

Spine — What rule holds this case upright?

The court reaffirmed the objective theory of contract:

A contract is formed when the parties' words and conduct, objectively assessed, show intention to be bound — not when they later change their minds.

This Spine stands in direct contrast to Gibson:

- Gibson = tentative language → no offer
- Storer = definitive language → offer + acceptance → contract

The Spine is clarity: Language that signals commitment creates legal obligation.

Brain — How does the court reason through this?

The court's reasoning is sharp and anatomical:

1. The Council's letter was not an invitation to treat.
2. It contained definite terms and a clear path to completion.
3. The phrase "I will send you the agreement signed…" shows commitment.
4. Storer's signature was acceptance, completing the contract.
5. The Council's later refusal was irrelevant — the contract already existed.

The Brain teaches students that administrative formalities do not prevent formation when intention is already clear.

Lungs — How does this doctrine expand or contract?

This case expands contract law by:

- Strengthening the objective theory of intention
- Emphasizing the power of clear, directive language
- Protecting individuals who rely on formal communications
- Reinforcing that political changes cannot undo completed contracts

It contracts the idea that a countersignature is always required for formation.

Stomach — The digestible takeaway

Students should walk away knowing:

- "If you sign, we will sign" is an offer.
- Storer's signature was acceptance.
- A contract formed before the Council changed its mind.
- Clear, definitive language creates binding obligations.

This case is the mirror image of Gibson — and that contrast is the lesson.

Skin — The holding

The court held:

- The Council's letter was an offer.
- Storer accepted by signing and returning the agreement.
- A binding contract existed.

- The Council was required to complete the sale.

Fractures — Cracks, tensions, and doctrinal shifts

- Highlights the tension between administrative procedure and contractual intention
- Shows how politics can collide with private expectations
- Demonstrates the limits of governmental flexibility once intention is expressed
- Reinforces the need for precision in public-body communications
- Creates a doctrinal pairing with Gibson that students must understand together

The fractures reveal the human stakes: Two men, two letters, two hopes — and two very different outcomes.

Case 8 — *Hyde v. Wrench (1840)*

Pulse — What happens when a counter-offer replaces a heartbeat?

This case begins with a negotiation over a farm. Wrench offered to sell his farm to Hyde for £1,000. Hyde replied with a counter-offer of £950.

Wrench refused. Hyde then tried to "accept" the original £1,000 offer.

But the Pulse of this case is the moment the counter-offer is made — a moment that kills the original offer.

The heartbeat of the first offer stops the instant a counter-offer is proposed.

Veins — How does offer and acceptance flow?

The circulation in this case is a lesson in fragility:

- Wrench made an offer of £1,000.
- Hyde made a counter-offer of £950.
- The counter-offer destroyed the original offer.
- When Hyde later tried to accept the £1,000 offer, it was too late — the offer no longer existed.

The Veins show that a counter-offer does not merely redirect the flow — it cuts it off entirely.

Muscle — What gives this agreement enforceable strength?

The Muscle is missing because:

- There was no existing offer to accept.

- Mutual assent requires both parties to agree to the same terms.
- Once Hyde introduced new terms, the original terms died.

The enforceable strength of a contract depends on matching intentions. Here, the intentions never aligned.

Heart — What is the core dispute?

Hyde argued:

- His later acceptance of the £1,000 offer created a binding contract.

Wrench argued:

- The £1,000 offer was terminated by Hyde's counter-offer.
- There was nothing left for Hyde to accept.

The Heart of the case is the question:

Does a counter-offer terminate the original offer?

The court said yes.

Spine — What rule holds this case upright?

The court established a foundational rule:

A counter-offer terminates the original offer. You cannot revive a dead offer by later accepting it.

This Spine is essential to negotiation:

- It prevents parties from "shopping around" between offers.
- It ensures clarity and finality in bargaining.
- It protects offerors from being bound after rejection.

Brain — How does the court reason through this?

The court reasoned with crisp logic:

1. Wrench offered to sell for £1,000.
2. Hyde rejected that offer by making a counter-offer of £950.
3. A counter-offer is a rejection of the original offer.
4. Once rejected, the original offer cannot be accepted.
5. Hyde's later attempt to accept £1,000 was ineffective.
6. Therefore, no contract existed.

The Brain teaches students that negotiation has consequences — every move matters.

Lungs — How does this doctrine expand or contract?

This case expands contract law by:

- Clarifying the effect of counter-offers
- Reinforcing the need for clear acceptance
- Protecting offerors from revived or zombie offers
- Teaching students the importance of precise negotiation strategy

It contracts the idea that parties can return to earlier offers at will.

Stomach — The digestible takeaway

Students should remember:

- A counter-offer = rejection of the original offer.
- You cannot later accept an offer you previously rejected.

- Negotiation resets the contractual landscape.
- Mutual assent requires matching terms at the same moment.

This case is the anatomy of how offers die.

Skin — The holding

The court held:

- Hyde's counter-offer terminated Wrench's original offer.
- Hyde could not later accept the £1,000 offer.
- No contract was formed.

Fractures — Cracks, tensions, and doctrinal shifts

- Highlights the delicate choreography of negotiation
- Shows how easily parties can lose an offer through miscalculation
- Reinforces the need for strategic communication
- Forms a doctrinal trio with Felthouse and Harvey v. Facey
- Reminds students that silence, hesitation, or counter-moves can reshape the entire deal

The fractures reveal the human element: one misstep in negotiation can close a door forever

Case 9 — *Felthouse v. Bindley (1862)*

Pulse — Can silence speak acceptance?

This case begins with an uncle who wanted to buy his nephew's horse. He wrote a letter saying:

"If I hear no more about him, I consider the horse mine at £30 15s."

A sentence full of assumption. A heartbeat that tries to turn silence into agreement.

But the Pulse here is the truth that silence has no voice in contract law — and cannot be forced to speak acceptance.

Veins — How does offer and acceptance flow?

The circulation in this case is a lesson in communication:

- The uncle made an offer.
- He attempted to impose acceptance through silence.
- The nephew never communicated acceptance.
- The auctioneer mistakenly sold the horse to someone else.

The Veins show that acceptance must flow outward, not remain unspoken.

Muscle — What gives this agreement enforceable strength?

The Muscle is missing because:

- Acceptance must be communicated.
- Silence cannot create mutual assent.

- One party cannot unilaterally dictate the method of acceptance.

Without a clear "yes," there is no contractual strength.

Heart — What is the core dispute?

Felthouse (the uncle) argued:

- His offer was accepted because the nephew did not object.
- The horse was already his when the auctioneer sold it.

Bindley (the auctioneer) argued:

- No contract existed between uncle and nephew.
- Therefore, he could not have sold the uncle's horse.

The Heart of the case is the question:

Can silence amount to acceptance?

The court said no.

Spine — What rule holds this case upright?

The court reaffirmed a foundational rule:

Silence cannot constitute acceptance. Acceptance must be communicated clearly and unequivocally.

This Spine protects:

- Autonomy
- Clarity
- Fairness in negotiation
- The right not to be bound by inaction

Brain — How does the court reason through this?

The court reasoned with firm logic:

1. The uncle attempted to impose acceptance by silence.
2. The nephew never communicated acceptance.
3. Without communication, there is no acceptance.
4. Without acceptance, there is no contract.
5. Therefore, the horse was not the uncle's property at the time of the sale.

The Brain teaches students that agreement requires expression, not assumption.

Lungs — How does this doctrine expand or contract?

This case expands contract law by:

- Reinforcing the need for communicated acceptance
- Protecting parties from being bound by silence
- Clarifying that offerors cannot dictate acceptance methods unilaterally
- Ensuring fairness in contractual formation

It contracts the idea that inaction can ever equal agreement.

Stomach — The digestible takeaway

Students should remember:

- Silence ≠ acceptance
- Acceptance must be communicated

- One party cannot impose acceptance terms on the other
- No communication = no contract

This case is the anatomy of why contracts require a clear "yes."

Skin — The holding

The court held:

- Silence did not amount to acceptance.
- No contract existed between uncle and nephew.
- The horse was not the uncle's property.
- The auctioneer was not liable.

Fractures — Cracks, tensions, and doctrinal shifts

- Highlights the tension between intention and communication
- Shows how easily assumptions can derail agreements
- Reinforces the importance of explicit acceptance
- Forms a doctrinal trio with Hyde and Harvey
- Reminds students that clarity is the lifeblood of contract formation

The fractures reveal the human truth: silence may feel meaningful, but in law, it says nothing.

Case 10 — *Balfour v. Balfour (1919)*

Pulse — What intention beats beneath the surface?

This case begins not in a marketplace or a boardroom, but in a marriage — a space filled with affection, routine, and private understandings.

Mr. Balfour worked overseas. Mrs. Balfour stayed in England for health reasons. He promised to send her **£30 a month** until she could join him.

At the time, it felt like a natural promise between spouses. But when the marriage broke down, Mrs. Balfour sued to enforce that promise.

The Pulse here is the question:

Do domestic promises carry the intention to create legal relations?

The heartbeat of this case is the difference between **love** and **law**.

Veins — How does offer and acceptance flow?

The Veins of this case show the flow of promises inside a relationship:

- Husband promises support
- Wife relies on it
- Both act as spouses, not as contracting parties
- No negotiation

- No formality
- No commercial context

The bloodstream of contract formation is present — but is it carrying legal intention, or just domestic goodwill?

Muscle — What gives this agreement enforceable strength?

Here is the key insight:

Domestic agreements lack the muscle of legal enforceability unless intention is clearly shown.

Why?

Because:

- Spouses make countless promises
- They are not meant to be litigated
- The law avoids intruding into private domestic arrangements
- There is no expectation of legal consequence

The Muscle is missing — not because the promise lacked sincerity, but because it lacked **legal intention**.

Heart — What is the core dispute?

The Heart of the case is the question:

Was Mr. Balfour's promise to pay £30 a month a legally binding contract?

If yes → he must pay. If no → it was a domestic arrangement

outside the reach of contract law.

Spine — What rule holds this case upright?

The court articulated a foundational rule:

Domestic or social agreements are presumed not to create legal relations.

This presumption can be rebutted — but not here.

This Spine becomes the backbone of intention doctrine.

Brain — How does the court reason through this?

The court's reasoning is gentle, realistic, and grounded in social understanding:

1. Spouses make many promises as part of daily life.
2. These promises are not intended to be legally enforceable.
3. The agreement was made in a moment of marital harmony.
4. There was no contemplation of legal consequences.
5. Once the marriage broke down, the context changed — but the original intention did not.
6. Therefore, no contract existed.

The Brain teaches students that **context shapes intention**, and the law respects the boundaries of private life.

Lungs — How does this doctrine expand or contract?

This case expands contract law by:

- Establishing the presumption against legal intention in domestic settings
- Protecting families from unnecessary litigation
- Clarifying the boundary between social promises and legal obligations

It contracts the idea that **every promise can be a contract**.

Stomach — The digestible takeaway

Students should walk away knowing:

- Domestic promises are **not** usually contracts.
- Intention to create legal relations must be clear.
- The law distinguishes between **home** and **commerce**.
- *Balfour v. Balfour* is the foundation of this distinction.

This case teaches the quiet wisdom of contract law.

Skin — The holding

The court held that:

- The agreement between Mr. and Mrs. Balfour was a **domestic arrangement**.
- There was **no intention to create legal relations**.
- Therefore, **no contract existed**.

Fractures — Cracks, tensions, and doctrinal shifts

- Critics argue the decision ignores the economic vulnerability of spouses.

- It raises questions about fairness when relationships break down.
- It contrasts sharply with *Merritt v. Merritt*, where intention *was* found.
- It foreshadows the evolution of family law and contractual intention.

The fractures make the doctrine more human — because relationships are human.

Case 11 — *Merritt v. Merritt* (1970)

Pulse — What intention beats beneath the surface?

This case begins where *Balfour* ends — not in harmony, but in fracture.

Mr. and Mrs. Merritt were no longer living together. Their marriage had broken down. They met to sort out finances, not affection. He agreed in writing to pay her **£40 a month**, and once the mortgage was paid off, he would **transfer the house into her name**.

This was not a promise made over breakfast. This was a promise made across emotional distance.

The Pulse here is unmistakable:

When a relationship has ended, promises are no longer domestic — they are legal.

Veins — How does offer and acceptance flow?

The Veins of this case carry the flow of negotiation, not marital goodwill:

- They met intentionally to settle financial matters.
- They discussed obligations and property.
- They wrote down the agreement.
- She relied on it and paid the mortgage.
- He later refused to transfer the house.

The bloodstream of contract formation is flowing with **clear intention**, not casual domesticity.

Muscle — What gives this agreement enforceable strength?

Here is the key insight:

When spouses are separated, their agreements usually carry legal intention.

The Muscle is strong because:

- The agreement was **written**.
- The context was **financial separation**, not affection.
- Mrs. Merritt provided **consideration** by paying the mortgage.
- Both parties intended to settle obligations permanently.

This is not a soft domestic promise — it is a structured agreement.

Heart — What is the core dispute?

The Heart of the case is the question:

Was the written agreement between the separated spouses intended to be legally binding?

If yes → the house must be transferred. If no → it was merely a domestic understanding.

Spine — What rule holds this case upright?

The court articulated a powerful counter-rule to *Balfour*:

****When spouses are separated or negotiating after breakdown,**

their agreements are presumed to create legal relations.**

This Spine recognizes the reality of human relationships — and their endings.

Brain — How does the court reason through this?

The court's reasoning is grounded in clarity and context:

1. The marriage had already broken down.
2. The parties were negotiating property and financial obligations.
3. The agreement was **written**, showing seriousness.
4. Mrs. Merritt relied on the agreement and paid the mortgage.
5. This was not a domestic arrangement — it was a **businesslike negotiation**.
6. Therefore, the agreement was intended to be legally binding.

The Brain teaches students that **context transforms intention**.

Lungs — How does this doctrine expand or contract?

This case expands contract law by:

- Recognizing legal intention in separated spouses
- Protecting vulnerable partners during financial negotiations
- Distinguishing between domestic harmony and post-breakdown agreements
- Reinforcing the importance of written promises

It contracts the idea that **all spousal promises are non-contractual**.

Stomach — The digestible takeaway

Students should walk away knowing:

- *Balfour v. Balfour* applies to **happy homes**.
- *Merritt v. Merritt* applies to **broken ones**.
- Separation changes everything — including intention.
- Written agreements between separated spouses are usually binding.

This case is the moment students understand that **intention lives in context**.

Skin — The holding

The court held that:

- The agreement was **intended to create legal relations**.
- Mrs. Merritt provided consideration by paying the mortgage.
- The promise to transfer the house was **enforceable**.
- The house must be transferred to her.

Fractures — Cracks, tensions, and doctrinal shifts

- It highlights the emotional complexity of family agreements.
- It draws a sharp line between domestic life and legal negotiation.
- It raises questions about fairness in marital breakdowns.

- It foreshadows modern family law's recognition of financial vulnerability.
- It shows how intention shifts with circumstance.

The fractures make the doctrine feel alive — because relationships are alive.

Case 12 — *Edwards v. Skyways Ltd* (1964)

Pulse — What intention beats beneath the surface?

This case begins in the world of aviation — a commercial environment where promises are made with calculators, not affection.

Skyways was making pilots redundant. To soften the blow, they agreed to pay an "ex gratia" payment — a goodwill sum — into the pilots' pension fund. Later, Skyways refused to pay, arguing:

"Ex gratia means we didn't intend to be legally bound."

But the Pulse of this case beats with a different rhythm:

In business, promises are presumed to be serious.

The heartbeat here is commercial intention — steady, deliberate, and enforceable.

Veins — How does offer and acceptance flow?

The Veins of this case carry the flow of a business negotiation:

- Skyways offered an ex gratia payment
- Edwards accepted the redundancy package on that basis
- He relied on the promise
- Skyways later tried to withdraw it

The bloodstream of contract formation is flowing with commercial intention, not domestic ambiguity.

Muscle — What gives this agreement enforceable strength?

Here is the key insight:

In commercial agreements, intention to create legal relations is presumed.

The Muscle is strong because:

- The context is business
- The promise was part of a redundancy negotiation
- Edwards relied on it
- Skyways gained the benefit of a smooth redundancy process

This is not a casual promise — it is a business commitment.

Heart — What is the core dispute?

The Heart of the case is the question:

Does the use of the phrase "ex gratia" remove legal intention from a commercial promise?

If yes → Skyways owes nothing. If no → the promise is binding.

Spine — What rule holds this case upright?

The court reaffirmed a foundational rule:

Commercial agreements are presumed to be legally binding unless clearly stated otherwise.

This Spine is the backbone of business contracting.

Brain — How does the court reason through this?

The court's reasoning is practical, commercial, and grounded in fairness:

1. The agreement was made in a business context.
2. The presumption of legal intention applies.
3. "Ex gratia" means without admitting liability, not without intention.
4. Skyways offered the payment to secure cooperation during redundancies.
5. Edwards relied on the promise.
6. Therefore, the promise is enforceable.

The Brain teaches students that words matter — but context matters more.

Lungs — How does this doctrine expand or contract?

This case expands contract law by:

- Reinforcing the presumption of intention in commercial settings
- Clarifying the meaning of "ex gratia"
- Protecting employees in redundancy negotiations
- Strengthening the reliability of business promises

It contracts the idea that labels alone can remove legal intention.

Stomach — The digestible takeaway

Students should walk away knowing:

- Business promises are presumed binding.

- "Ex gratia" does not cancel legal intention.
- Commercial context creates enforceability.
- *Edwards v. Skyways* is the cornerstone of intention in business agreements.

This case is the moment students understand the difference between domestic promises and commercial commitments.

Skin — The holding

The court held that:

- The agreement was made in a commercial context.
- The presumption of legal intention applied.
- "Ex gratia" did not negate intention.
- Skyways was legally bound to pay the sum.

Fractures — Cracks, tensions, and doctrinal shifts

- It highlights the contrast between domestic and commercial intention.
- It raises questions about the power imbalance in redundancy negotiations.
- It shows how labels like "ex gratia" can be misunderstood.
- It foreshadows modern employment law protections.
- It reinforces the idea that context shapes intention.

The fractures make the doctrine richer — because business relationships are complex.

3. Certainty & Completeness

Case 13 — *Scammell v. Ouston* (1941)

Pulse — What intention beats beneath the surface?

This case begins with two parties who genuinely wanted to make a deal.

Ouston wanted to buy a new van. Scammell agreed in principle. The parties wrote that the purchase would be made:

"On hire-purchase terms."

To them, this phrase felt familiar — a shorthand they both understood in their own commercial world.

But to the court, the Pulse of the agreement was faint. The question became:

Did the parties intend a legally binding contract if the key term was so vague?

The heartbeat here is the tension between **good intentions** and **uncertain language**.

Veins — How does offer and acceptance flow?

The Veins of this case show the flow of negotiation:

- Ouston offered to buy the van.
- Scammell accepted — but only "on hire-purchase terms."
- No specific terms were ever agreed upon.
- When the deal fell apart, Ouston sued to enforce the agreement.

The bloodstream of contract formation is flowing — but the blood lacks oxygen. The essential terms are missing.

Muscle — What gives this agreement enforceable strength?

Here is the key insight:

A contract must have sufficiently certain terms to be enforceable.

The Muscle is weak because:

- "Hire-purchase terms" could mean many different things.
- No specific repayment schedule was agreed.
- No interest rate.
- No duration.
- No standard form was referenced.

Without certainty, the contract has no muscle — it cannot stand.

Heart — What is the core dispute?

The Heart of the case is the question:

Is an agreement to buy a van "on hire-purchase terms" too vague to enforce?

If yes → no contract exists. If no → the court must enforce the deal.

Spine — What rule holds this case upright?

The court reaffirmed a foundational rule:

A contract must be sufficiently certain in its essential terms.

Vague or incomplete terms cannot be enforced.**

This Spine protects parties from being bound by unclear agreements.

Brain — How does the court reason through this?

The court's reasoning is careful, practical, and grounded in the need for clarity:

1. "Hire-purchase terms" is not a single, fixed concept.
2. Different companies use different forms and conditions.
3. The court cannot guess what the parties intended.
4. Courts enforce agreements — they do not write them.
5. Without clear terms, there is no contract.

The Brain teaches students that **certainty is not a luxury — it is a requirement**.

Lungs — How does this doctrine expand or contract?

This case expands contract law by:

- Clarifying the need for certainty in essential terms
- Protecting parties from ambiguous agreements
- Reinforcing the court's role as interpreter, not creator

It contracts the idea that **good intentions alone can form a contract**.

Stomach — The digestible takeaway

Students should walk away knowing:

- A contract must have **clear, definite terms**.
- Vague phrases like "on hire-purchase terms" are not enough.
- Courts will not fill in essential terms.
- *Scammell v. Ouston* is the cornerstone of certainty doctrine.

This case teaches the quiet discipline of precision in contracting.

Skin — The holding

The court held that:

- The phrase "on hire-purchase terms" was **too vague**.
- The essential terms were not agreed.
- Therefore, **no contract existed**.

Fractures — Cracks, tensions, and doctrinal shifts

- Critics argue the court could have implied standard terms.
- It raises questions about commercial custom and usage.
- It contrasts sharply with cases where courts *do* imply terms.
- It foreshadows the tension between certainty and flexibility in modern contracting.

The fractures make the doctrine richer — because language is imperfect.

Case 14 — *Hillas v. Arcos* (1932)

Pulse — What intention beats beneath the surface?

This case begins with two companies who had done business

before — real, ongoing, commercial partners.

In 1930, Hillas bought timber from Arcos. The contract included an option for Hillas to buy more timber the next year "of fair specification."

That phrase — "fair specification" — is vague on its face. But beneath it beats a strong commercial Pulse:

These parties had a history. They knew each other's standards. They intended to keep doing business.

This is not a casual or uncertain promise. It is a continuation of a commercial relationship.

Veins — How does offer and acceptance flow?

The Veins of this case carry the flow of a long-term business arrangement:

- Hillas bought timber in 1930.
- The contract gave them an option for 1931.
- They exercised the option.
- Arcos refused to supply.
- Hillas sued.

The bloodstream of contract formation is flowing through **commercial continuity**, not isolated negotiation.

Muscle — What gives this agreement enforceable strength?

Here is the key insight:

Commercial context can supply missing details.

The Muscle is strong because:

- The parties had a prior course of dealing.
- They had used similar terms before.
- The industry had standard practices.
- The option clause was part of a larger, structured contract.

This is not vague in the way *Scammell* was vague. This is **incomplete but interpretable**.

Heart — What is the core dispute?

The Heart of the case is the question:

Was the option clause too vague ("fair specification") to be enforceable?

If yes → Arcos owes nothing. If no → the court must enforce the option.

Spine — What rule holds this case upright?

The court articulated a flexible, commercial rule:

****Courts should interpret commercial agreements in a way that gives effect to the parties' intentions,**

especially when there is a prior course of dealing.**

This Spine is the backbone of modern commercial certainty.

Brain — How does the court reason through this?

The court's reasoning is practical, business-savvy, and deeply respectful of commercial reality:

1. The parties had done business before.
2. They understood what "fair specification" meant between them.
3. The option clause was part of a larger, detailed contract.
4. Commercial agreements should be interpreted, not destroyed.
5. Courts should strive to uphold bargains, not defeat them.
6. The missing terms could be supplied by industry standards and prior dealings.

The Brain teaches students that **certainty is contextual, not mechanical.**

Lungs — How does this doctrine expand or contract?

This case expands contract law by:

- Allowing courts to imply terms from context
- Recognizing commercial relationships as sources of certainty
- Encouraging stability in long-term business dealings
- Softening the rigidity of the certainty doctrine

It contracts the idea that **every vague term is fatal.**

Stomach — The digestible takeaway

Students should walk away knowing:

- Courts enforce commercial agreements whenever possible.

- Prior dealings can supply missing terms.
- "Fair specification" was vague, but not fatally so.
- *Hillas v. Arcos* is the flexible counterpart to *Scammell v. Ouston.*

This case teaches the art of **interpreting**, not destroying, agreements.

Skin — The holding

The court held that:

- The option clause was **sufficiently certain** when read in commercial context.
- The missing terms could be supplied by prior dealings and industry standards.
- Arcos breached the contract by refusing to supply the timber.

Fractures — Cracks, tensions, and doctrinal shifts

- It highlights the tension between strict certainty and commercial practicality.
- It raises questions about how far courts should go in implying terms.
- It contrasts sharply with *Scammell*, showing the doctrine's flexibility.
- It foreshadows modern approaches to interpretation and implied terms.
- It shows that **certainty is not about perfect wording — it's about workable intention**.

The fractures make the doctrine feel alive — because business is alive.

Part II. Misrepresentation

4. Fraudulent Misrepresentation

Case 15 — *Derry v. Peek (1889)*

Pulse — When does a false statement become fraud?

This case begins with a tramway company seeking permission to use steam-powered trams. Their prospectus confidently stated that they *had* the right to use steam power — but in truth, they only had permission subject to approval by the Board of Trade.

The approval never came. The company collapsed. Investors sued.

The Pulse here is the tension between honest mistake and fraudulent misrepresentation — between optimism and deceit.

Veins — How does misrepresentation flow?

The circulation in this case runs through three possible states of mind:

- Knowing the statement is false
- Not caring whether it is true or false (recklessness)
- Honestly believing it is true

Only the first two amount to fraud.

The Veins show that liability for deceit requires a specific mental state, not merely an incorrect statement.

Muscle — What gives this agreement enforceable strength?

The Muscle of a deceit claim lies in proving:

- A false representation
- Made knowingly, recklessly, or without belief in its truth

- Intended to induce reliance
- Actually relied upon
- Causing loss

In Derry v. Peek, the directors honestly believed their statement. That honest belief — even if careless — removes the muscle needed for fraud.

Heart — What is the core dispute?

The investors argued:

- The prospectus falsely stated that steam power was authorized.
- The directors' statement induced investment.
- The falsehood amounted to fraudulent misrepresentation.

The directors argued:

- They genuinely believed approval was a mere formality.
- They had no intention to deceive.
- At worst, they were negligent — not fraudulent.

The Heart of the case is the question:

Does an honestly held but mistaken belief amount to fraud?

The court said no.

Spine — What rule holds this case upright?

The House of Lords established the classic definition of fraud:

Fraud exists only when a false statement is made knowingly, without belief in its truth, or recklessly without caring whether it is true or false.

Negligence is not enough. Optimism is not enough. Mistake is not enough.

This Spine stands at the center of misrepresentation doctrine.

Brain — How does the court reason through this?

The court reasoned with strict logic:

1. Fraud requires actual dishonesty.
2. The directors believed approval was certain.
3. Their belief, though mistaken, was honest.
4. Honest belief defeats a claim of deceit.
5. Therefore, the investors could not recover under the tort of deceit.

The Brain teaches students that fraud is about state of mind, not outcome.

Lungs — How does this doctrine expand or contract?

This case expands contract and tort law by:

- Setting a high threshold for fraud
- Protecting honest business judgment
- Distinguishing negligence from deceit
- Clarifying that liability depends on intention, not error

It contracts the scope of investor protection under common law fraud.

Stomach — The digestible takeaway

Students should remember:

- Fraud = dishonesty
- Honest mistake ≠ fraud
- Recklessness = fraud
- Negligence ≠ fraud
- Derry v. Peek sets the classic test for fraudulent misrepresentation

This case is the anatomy of why proving fraud is difficult.

Skin — The holding

The court held:

- The directors honestly believed their statement.
- There was no fraud.
- The investors' claim for deceit failed.
- No damages were awarded.

Fractures — Cracks, tensions, and doctrinal shifts

- Critics argue the standard is too protective of companies
- Highlights the gap between moral blame and legal liability
- Led to the development of negligent misrepresentation in later cases (e.g., Hedley Byrne)
- Shows the limits of common law fraud before statutory reform
- Demonstrates how investor reliance was historically under-protected

The fractures reveal the human cost of optimism mistaken for certainty.

5. Negligent Misstatement

Case 16 — *Hedley Byrne & Co Ltd v. Heller & Partners Ltd (1964)*

Pulse — When does careless advice become legal responsibility?

This case begins with an advertising agency, Hedley Byrne, considering whether to extend credit to a client. Before doing so, they sought reassurance from the client's bank, Heller & Partners.

The bank replied with a reference that suggested the client was financially sound — but added a small, powerful disclaimer:

"Without responsibility on the part of this bank."

The client collapsed. Hedley Byrne suffered losses. They sued the bank for negligent misstatement.

The Pulse here is the emergence of a new question in contract and tort:

Can someone be liable for careless words, even without a contract?

Veins — How does liability flow?

The circulation in this case runs through a new channel:

- No contract existed between Hedley Byrne and the bank.
- No fraud was alleged.
- The claim was based on negligence — careless words causing financial loss.
- The court recognized a duty of care in giving advice or information in certain relationships.

But the disclaimer cut the flow short.

The Veins show that liability for statements can arise outside contract, but only when responsibility is assumed.

Muscle — What gives this agreement enforceable strength?

The Muscle of negligent misstatement lies in four elements:

- A special relationship creating a duty of care
- Reliance on the statement
- Reasonableness of that reliance
- Carelessness in making the statement

In this case, the relationship between bank and inquirer was close enough to create potential liability — but the disclaimer removed the muscle needed to enforce it.

Heart — What is the core dispute?

Hedley Byrne argued:

- The bank's reference was negligent.
- They relied on it.
- The bank should compensate them for their loss.

Heller argued:

- They owed no duty of care.
- Their disclaimer excluded responsibility.
- They could not be liable for reliance on a statement they expressly disowned.

The Heart of the case is the question:

Can negligent misstatements create liability in the absence of a contract?

The court said yes — in principle.

But not here.

Spine — What rule holds this case upright?

The House of Lords established a landmark rule:

A duty of care arises when a party gives advice or information in circumstances where they know it will be relied upon, and they voluntarily assume responsibility for its accuracy.

However:

A clear disclaimer can prevent that duty from arising.

This Spine reshaped modern tort law.

Brain — How does the court reason through this?

The court reasoned with doctrinal innovation:

1. Negligent misstatement can create liability even without a contract.
2. A "special relationship" arises when responsibility is assumed.
3. The bank's reference was given in a context that could create such a relationship.
4. But the disclaimer — "without responsibility" — prevented any duty of care.
5. Therefore, the bank was not liable, even though the statement was relied upon.

The Brain teaches students that words can carry legal weight, but disclaimers can lift that weight away.

Lungs — How does this doctrine expand or contract?

This case expands tort law by:

- Recognizing negligent misstatement as a source of liability
- Creating the concept of a "special relationship"
- Bridging the gap between contract and tort
- Protecting reliance on professional advice

It contracts liability where disclaimers are clear and effective.

Stomach — The digestible takeaway

Students should remember:

- Negligent misstatement can create liability without a contract
- A "special relationship" + reliance = duty of care
- Disclaimers can defeat that duty
- Hedley Byrne is the foundation of modern professional negligence

This case is the anatomy of how careless words can cause legal consequences.

Skin — The holding

The court held:

- A duty of care for negligent misstatement can exist.
- But the bank's disclaimer prevented such a duty here.

- Therefore, the bank was not liable.
- Hedley Byrne's claim failed.

Fractures — Cracks, tensions, and doctrinal shifts

- Introduces the concept of assumption of responsibility
- Blurs the boundary between contract and tort
- Raises questions about the power of disclaimers
- Lays the groundwork for modern professional liability
- Marks a turning point in the law of economic loss

The fractures reveal a legal system evolving to meet the realities of modern reliance.

6. Statutory Misrepresentation (Misrepresentation Act 1967)

Case 17 — Howard Marine & Dredging Co Ltd v. Ogden (1978)

Pulse — When does a mistaken statement become negligent misrepresentation?

This case begins with a simple question about capacity. Ogden wanted to hire barges from Howard Marine. They asked how much each barge could carry.

Howard Marine's representative confidently stated the capacity as 1,600 tonnes, relying on a figure from a Lloyd's Register entry — a respected industry source.

But the true capacity, listed in the actual ship documents, was only 1,000 tonnes.

Ogden suffered losses and refused to pay. Howard Marine sued. Ogden counterclaimed for negligent misrepresentation.

The Pulse here is the tension between reasonable reliance on industry sources and the duty to check primary documents.

Veins — How does liability flow?

The circulation in this case runs through the Misrepresentation Act 1967:

- A false statement was made.
- It induced Ogden to enter the contract.
- The burden shifted to Howard Marine to prove reasonable grounds for believing the statement was true.

The Veins show that under the Act, the representor must justify their belief — and industry custom is not always enough.

Muscle — What gives this agreement enforceable strength?

The Muscle of Ogden's claim lies in:

- A clear, factual representation (barge capacity)
- Reliance by Ogden
- Loss suffered
- Failure by Howard Marine to show reasonable grounds for their belief

The court held that relying on Lloyd's Register was not reasonable when the official ship documents were available and contradicted it.

The muscle of liability grew from the company's failure to check the most authoritative source.

Heart — What is the core dispute?

Ogden argued:

- Howard Marine's statement about capacity was false.
- They relied on it.
- The misrepresentation was negligent under the 1967 Act.

Howard Marine argued:

- They honestly believed the Lloyd's Register figure.
- The mistake was understandable.
- They had reasonable grounds for their belief.

The Heart of the case is the question:

Is reliance on an industry register reasonable when primary documents say otherwise?

The court said no.

Spine — What rule holds this case upright?

The Court of Appeal established a key rule:

Under the Misrepresentation Act 1967, the representor must show reasonable grounds for believing their statement was true. Industry custom is not enough when better evidence is available.

This Spine reinforces:

- The importance of primary documents
- The burden-shifting nature of the Act
- The high standard of care in commercial representations

Brain — How does the court reason through this?

The court reasoned with sharp logic:

1. A false statement was made about barge capacity.
2. Ogden relied on it when entering the contract.
3. Under the 1967 Act, Howard Marine had to prove reasonable grounds for belief.
4. They relied on Lloyd's Register, but the official ship documents contradicted it.
5. The official documents were the most authoritative source.
6. Failing to check them was unreasonable.
7. Therefore, the misrepresentation was negligent.

The Brain teaches students that commercial representations demand diligence.

Lungs — How does this doctrine expand or contract?

This case expands misrepresentation law by:

- Clarifying the burden of proof under the 1967 Act
- Emphasizing the need to verify information using primary sources
- Strengthening protection for parties relying on factual statements

It contracts the idea that honest belief alone is enough to avoid liability.

Stomach — The digestible takeaway

Students should remember:

- Under the Misrepresentation Act, the representor must prove reasonable grounds.
- Honest belief ≠ reasonable belief.
- Primary documents outrank industry registers.
- Failure to check authoritative sources = negligence.

This case is the anatomy of commercial carelessness.

Skin — The holding

The court held:

- Howard Marine's reliance on Lloyd's Register was not reasonable.

- They failed to discharge the burden under the 1967 Act.
- Ogden succeeded in their counterclaim for negligent misrepresentation.
- Damages were awarded.

Fractures — Cracks, tensions, and doctrinal shifts

- Highlights tension between industry practice and legal standards
- Shows the strictness of the Misrepresentation Act's burden-shifting
- Reinforces the primacy of official documents
- Demonstrates the limits of "honest mistake" after Derry v. Peek
- Forms a doctrinal bridge between negligent misstatement and statutory misrepresentation

The fractures reveal a commercial world where good faith is not enough — diligence is required.

7. Reliance & the Right to Rescind

Case 18 — *Redgrave v. Hurd (1881)*

Pulse — How far does a party's right to rely on a representation extend?

This case begins with a solicitor, Redgrave, who wished to take on a partner. He showed Hurd a set of papers suggesting the practice earned **£300 a year**. He also stated that additional papers — which Hurd did not inspect — would confirm the income.

In truth, the practice earned far less.

Hurd later discovered the truth and refused to complete the partnership agreement. Redgrave sued for specific performance. Hurd counterclaimed for rescission.

The Pulse here is the question:

Must a representee verify a statement, or may they rely on it at face value?

The court said they may rely.

Veins — How does reliance flow?

The circulation in this case is direct:

- A false representation was made.
- It induced Hurd to enter the contract.
- Hurd *could* have discovered the truth by checking the papers.
- But he was **not required** to do so.

The Veins show that reliance flows freely unless the representee **actually knows** the truth.

Muscle — What gives this agreement enforceable strength?

The Muscle of Hurd's right to rescind lies in:

- **A material misrepresentation**
- **Inducement**
- **No duty to investigate**
- **Prompt action upon discovery**

The court emphasized that the representee's failure to check documents does **not** defeat the right to rescind.

The muscle is the principle that **trust is protected**.

Heart — What is the core dispute?

Redgrave argued:

- Hurd should have checked the papers.
- His failure to investigate broke the chain of reliance.
- Therefore, rescission should be denied.

Hurd argued:

- He relied on Redgrave's statements.
- He was entitled to do so.
- The misrepresentation entitled him to rescind.

The Heart of the case is the question:

Does the right to rescind survive when the representee could have discovered the truth?

The court said yes.

Spine — What rule holds this case upright?

The court established a powerful rule:

A representee is entitled to rely on a material representation and is under no duty to verify it.

This Spine protects:

- Trust in negotiations
- Vulnerable parties
- The integrity of representations

Brain — How does the court reason through this?

The court reasoned with clarity:

1. A false representation was made about the practice's income.
2. Hurd relied on it when entering the contract.
3. The fact that he *could* have discovered the truth is irrelevant.
4. The law does not require investigation.
5. Therefore, Hurd was entitled to rescind.

The Brain teaches students that **misrepresentation protects reliance, not diligence**.

Lungs — How does this doctrine expand or contract?

This case expands misrepresentation law by:

- Strengthening the right to rely on statements
- Removing any duty to investigate

- Protecting representees from subtle blame-shifting

It contracts the idea that "you should have checked" is a valid defense.

Stomach — The digestible takeaway

Students should remember:

- No duty to investigate
- Reliance is presumed when a material statement is made
- Misrepresentation gives a right to rescind
- Redgrave v. Hurd is the backbone of reliance doctrine

Skin — The holding

The court held:

- Hurd relied on the misrepresentation.
- He was entitled to rescind.
- Redgrave's claim for specific performance failed.

Fractures — Cracks, tensions, and doctrinal shifts

- Highlights tension between fairness and personal responsibility
- Reinforces the protective nature of misrepresentation law
- Forms a doctrinal trio with **Leaf** and **Caldwell**
- Shows the limits of "caveat emptor" in modern contract law

The fractures reveal a legal system that values trust over suspicion.

Case 19 — *Leaf v. International Galleries (1950)*

Pulse — When does the right to rescind quietly expire?

This case begins with a painting. Leaf purchased what he believed — based on the gallery's representation — to be a work by **John Constable**, a famous English landscape artist.

Five years later, he discovered the truth: The painting was **not** by Constable.

Leaf sought to rescind the contract and recover the purchase price.

But the Pulse here is the quiet, ticking heartbeat of **lapse of time** — the idea that even a valid right to rescind can fade if not exercised promptly.

Veins — How does reliance and rescission flow?

The circulation in this case is subtle:

- A representation was made: "This is a Constable."
- Leaf relied on it.
- The representation was false.
- But Leaf waited **five years** before seeking rescission.

The Veins show that misrepresentation gives a right to rescind — but that right must be exercised **within a reasonable time**, especially when the misrepresentation goes to **quality**, not identity.

Muscle — What gives this agreement enforceable strength?

The Muscle of Leaf's claim lies in:

- A **material misrepresentation**

- **Inducement**
- **Reliance**

But the muscle weakens because:

- The misrepresentation was **innocent**, not fraudulent
- The right to rescind is **equitable**, not automatic
- Equity requires **promptness**

The muscle collapses under the weight of delay.

Heart — What is the core dispute?

Leaf argued:

- The painting was misdescribed.
- The misrepresentation induced the purchase.
- He should be allowed to rescind and recover the price.

International Galleries argued:

- Too much time had passed.
- The right to rescind had lapsed.
- At most, Leaf might have a claim for damages — but not rescission.

The Heart of the case is the question:

Can a buyer rescind a contract for innocent misrepresentation after a long delay?

The court said no.

Spine — What rule holds this case upright?

The court established a key rule:

The right to rescind for innocent misrepresentation is lost if not exercised within a reasonable time.

This Spine reinforces:

- Equity's demand for prompt action
- The distinction between innocent and fraudulent misrepresentation
- The finality of completed transactions

Brain — How does the court reason through this?

The court reasoned with equitable clarity:

1. The gallery's statement was an **innocent misrepresentation**.
2. Rescission is an equitable remedy.
3. Equity requires rescission to be sought **promptly**.
4. Five years is far too long.
5. The contract was fully executed — the painting had changed hands.
6. Therefore, the right to rescind was lost.

The Brain teaches students that **equity aids the vigilant, not the sleeping**.

Lungs — How does this doctrine expand or contract?

This case expands misrepresentation law by:

- Clarifying the limits of rescission

- Emphasizing the importance of timing
- Distinguishing between innocent and fraudulent misrepresentation

It contracts the availability of rescission for long-delayed claims.

Stomach — The digestible takeaway

Students should remember:

- Innocent misrepresentation gives a right to rescind
- But that right can be lost through **delay**
- Rescission is equitable, not automatic
- Leaf v. International Galleries is the classic case on **lapse of time**

Skin — The holding

The court held:

- The misrepresentation was innocent.
- Leaf waited too long to rescind.
- The right to rescind had lapsed.
- The contract stood.

Fractures — Cracks, tensions, and doctrinal shifts

- Highlights the tension between fairness and finality
- Shows how equity tempers contractual remedies
- Demonstrates the limits of buyer protection

- Forms a doctrinal bridge between **Redgrave** (broad right to rely) and **Caldwell** (rescission without communication)
- Raises questions about art attribution and commercial certainty

The fractures reveal a legal truth: even valid rights can fade if left unused.

Case 20 — *Car & Universal Finance Co Ltd v. Caldwell (1965)*

Pulse — Can rescission occur without telling the other party?

This case begins with a car owner, Mr. Caldwell, who sold his Jaguar to a man named Hirachand. The buyer paid with a **fraudulent cheque** and immediately disappeared with the car.

Caldwell acted quickly:

- He notified the police
- He notified the Automobile Association
- He attempted to recover the car

But he could not contact the fraudulent buyer.

Later, the car was sold on to an innocent third party, Car & Universal Finance.

The Pulse here is the urgent question:

Can a contract be rescinded when communication with the fraudulent party is impossible?

The court said yes.

Veins — How does rescission flow?

The circulation in this case runs through the doctrine of **rescission ab initio**:

- Fraudulent misrepresentation gives the right to rescind
- Rescission normally requires **communication**
- But fraudsters often vanish
- Equity will not allow fraud to defeat rescission

The Veins show that rescission can flow through **actions**, not words.

Muscle — What gives this agreement enforceable strength?

The Muscle of Caldwell's rescission lies in:

- **Fraudulent misrepresentation** by the buyer
- **Prompt action** by Caldwell
- **Clear intention** to rescind
- **Objective steps** taken to undo the contract

The court held that these steps were enough to **effectively rescind**, even without communication.

The muscle is the principle that **fraud does not freeze the victim**.

Heart — What is the core dispute?

Car & Universal Finance argued:

- They bought the car in good faith.
- Caldwell had not rescinded before the car passed to them.
- Therefore, title had transferred.

Caldwell argued:

- He rescinded the contract as soon as he discovered the fraud.
- His inability to contact the fraudster should not defeat rescission.
- Title never passed to the fraudulent buyer.

The Heart of the case is the question:

Is rescission effective without communication when the other party has made communication impossible?

The court said yes.

Spine — What rule holds this case upright?

The court established a powerful rule:

When a contract is induced by fraud, rescission can be effected by any unequivocal act showing an intention to rescind, even without communication, if communication is impossible due to the fraudster's conduct.

This Spine protects victims of fraud and prevents fraudsters from laundering title.

Brain — How does the court reason through this?

The court reasoned with equitable precision:

1. Fraud gives the right to rescind.
2. Rescission normally requires communication.
3. But the law will not allow a fraudster to avoid rescission by disappearing.
4. Caldwell took **clear, prompt, objective steps** to rescind.
5. These steps were sufficient to rescind the contract.
6. Because the contract was rescinded before the car reached Car & Universal, the fraudster never had good title to pass on.

The Brain teaches students that **equity adapts to prevent injustice**.

Lungs — How does this doctrine expand or contract?

This case expands rescission law by:

- Allowing rescission without communication
- Protecting victims of fraud
- Preventing fraudsters from passing good title
- Recognizing "unequivocal acts" as substitutes for notice

It contracts the strict requirement of communication in cases of fraud.

Stomach — The digestible takeaway

Students should remember:

- Fraudulent misrepresentation gives a right to rescind
- Rescission normally requires communication
- But if the fraudster disappears, **communication is not required**
- Any clear act showing intention to rescind is enough
- Caldwell is the classic case on **rescission without communication**

Skin — The holding

The court held:

- Caldwell effectively rescinded the contract by notifying the police and AA.
- Rescission occurred before the car reached Car & Universal.
- The fraudster never had good title.

- Car & Universal could not acquire good title.
- Caldwell retained ownership.

Fractures — Cracks, tensions, and doctrinal shifts

- Highlights tension between protecting innocent third parties and victims of fraud
- Shows equity's flexibility in the face of wrongdoing
- Reinforces the principle that fraud unravels all
- Completes the doctrinal arc begun in Redgrave and Leaf
- Demonstrates the law's refusal to let fraudsters exploit procedural rules

The fractures reveal a legal truth: **fraud does not get the last word — equity does.**

Part III. Remedies

8. Remoteness & Foreseeability

Case 21— *Hadley v. Baxendale* (1854)

Pulse — What intention beats beneath the surface?

This case begins with a broken mill — literally.

Hadley's mill shaft snapped. He hired Baxendale, a carrier, to deliver the broken shaft to engineers so they could make a replacement. Baxendale delayed the delivery. The mill stayed closed. Hadley lost profits.

He sued for those lost profits.

But beneath this simple story beats a deeper question:

When a contract is breached, which losses can the injured party recover?

The Pulse here is the tension between **fair compensation** and **predictable liability**.

Veins — How does offer and acceptance flow?

The Veins of this case carry the flow of expectations:

- Hadley expected timely delivery.
- Baxendale expected a routine shipment.
- Neither discussed the mill's shutdown.
- Neither discussed potential lost profits.
- The carrier had no idea the mill would be idle until the shaft returned.

The bloodstream of contract formation is flowing — but the question is whether the loss was within that flow.

Muscle — What gives this agreement enforceable strength?

Here is the key insight:

Damages must be within the reasonable contemplation of the parties at the time of contracting.

The Muscle of the damages claim is weak because:

- Baxendale did not know the mill would stop operating.
- The loss was not foreseeable.
- The risk was not allocated in the contract.

Without foreseeability, the damages claim has no muscle.

Heart — What is the core dispute?

The Heart of the case is the question:

Can Hadley recover lost profits when Baxendale did not know the mill would be shut down?

If yes → carriers face enormous, unpredictable liability. If no → Hadley bears the loss himself.

Spine — What rule holds this case upright?

The court articulated the foundational rule of remoteness:

****Damages are recoverable only if they:**

1. Arise naturally from the breach (ordinary course), OR

2. Were within the reasonable contemplation of both parties at the time of contracting.**

This Spine supports nearly every modern damages case.

Brain — How does the court reason through this?

The court's reasoning is elegant, balanced, and deeply practical:

1. Baxendale did not know the mill would be shut down.
2. The loss of profits was not a natural or obvious consequence.
3. The carrier could not foresee the magnitude of the loss.
4. Parties must be able to predict their potential liability.
5. Without foreseeability, damages become unbounded.
6. Therefore, the lost profits were too remote.

The Brain teaches students that **contract damages are about predictability, not punishment**.

Lungs — How does this doctrine expand or contract?

This case expands contract law by:

- Establishing the two-limb test for remoteness
- Protecting parties from unforeseeable liability
- Encouraging clear communication of special circumstances
- Creating a predictable framework for damages

It contracts the idea that **all losses caused by breach are recoverable**.

Stomach — The digestible takeaway

Students should walk away knowing:

- Damages must be **foreseeable**.
- Losses must be within the **reasonable contemplation** of both parties.
- Special circumstances must be **communicated** to be recoverable.
- *Hadley v. Baxendale* is the foundation of remoteness doctrine.

This case teaches the quiet discipline of fairness and predictability in contract remedies.

Skin — The holding

The court held that:

- The lost profits were **not foreseeable**.
- Baxendale did not know the mill would be shut down.
- The loss was too remote.
- Therefore, **Hadley could not recover lost profits**.

Fractures — Cracks, tensions, and doctrinal shifts

- Critics argue the rule can be harsh on innocent plaintiffs.
- It raises questions about how much communication is required.
- It contrasts with modern doctrines like assumption of responsibility.

- It foreshadows the evolution of foreseeability in cases like *Victoria Laundry* and *The Heron II*.
- It highlights the tension between **compensation** and **predictability**.

The fractures make the doctrine richer — because loss is complex.

Case 22 — *Victoria Laundry (Windsor) Ltd v. Newman Industries* (1949)

Pulse — What intention beats beneath the surface?

This case begins with a laundry business eager to expand. Victoria Laundry purchased a large boiler from Newman Industries. The boiler was essential — without it, they couldn't take on lucrative dyeing contracts.

Newman delayed delivery by **five months**.

Victoria Laundry lost:

- Ordinary profits from everyday laundry work
- Extraordinary profits from a highly lucrative government dyeing contract

The Pulse here is the tension between **ordinary commercial expectation** and **special, undisclosed opportunities**.

Veins — How does offer and acceptance flow?

The Veins of this case carry the flow of commercial reliance:

- Victoria Laundry bought the boiler for business expansion
- Newman knew the boiler was needed urgently
- Newman did **not** know about the special government contract
- The delay caused two types of loss

The bloodstream of contract formation is flowing — but the question is which losses were within that flow.

Muscle — What gives this agreement enforceable strength?

Here is the key insight:

Foreseeability depends on what the defendant knew — or ought to have known — at the time of contracting.

The Muscle is strong for ordinary losses because:

- Newman knew the boiler was for business use
- They knew delay would cause lost profits
- These losses were foreseeable

But the Muscle is weak for extraordinary losses because:

- Newman had no knowledge of the special contract
- The loss was not within their contemplation

Heart — What is the core dispute?

The Heart of the case is the question:

Can Victoria Laundry recover both ordinary and extraordinary lost profits?

If yes → foreseeability becomes extremely broad. If no → the law draws a line between ordinary and special losses.

Spine — What rule holds this case upright?

The court refined *Hadley* by articulating a practical rule:

A defendant is liable for losses that are:

1. Reasonably foreseeable as a serious possibility, and

2. Within their knowledge at the time of contracting.**

This Spine adds nuance to the *Hadley* test.

Brain — How does the court reason through this?

The court's reasoning is nuanced and commercially realistic:

1. Newman knew the boiler was for business use.
2. They knew delay would cause ordinary lost profits.
3. These losses were foreseeable — and recoverable.
4. But Newman did **not** know about the special government contract.
5. Extraordinary losses require **actual knowledge**.
6. Therefore, the special profits were too remote.

The Brain teaches students that **foreseeability is not one-size-fits-all**.

Lungs — How does this doctrine expand or contract?

This case expands contract law by:

- Introducing the idea of **ordinary vs. extraordinary losses**
- Clarifying the level of foreseeability required
- Making the *Hadley* test more flexible and realistic
- Protecting defendants from unforeseeable, exceptional liability

It contracts the idea that **all lost profits are treated the same**.

Stomach — The digestible takeaway

Students should walk away knowing:

- Ordinary lost profits are recoverable if foreseeable.
- Extraordinary profits require **actual knowledge**.
- Foreseeability depends on what the defendant knew at the time of contracting.
- *Victoria Laundry* refines and humanizes *Hadley v. Baxendale*.

This case teaches the art of distinguishing between **normal business loss** and **special opportunity loss**.

Skin — The holding

The court held that:

- Victoria Laundry could recover **ordinary lost profits**.
- They could **not** recover extraordinary profits from the special contract.
- The special loss was too remote.

Fractures — Cracks, tensions, and doctrinal shifts

- It raises questions about how much disclosure is required in commercial negotiations.
- It highlights the tension between fairness and predictability.
- It foreshadows *The Heron II*, which further refines foreseeability.
- It shows the evolution from rigid rules to nuanced commercial reasoning.

The fractures make the doctrine richer — because business is unpredictable.

Case 23 — The Heron II (Koufos v. C Czarnikow Ltd) (1969)

Pulse — What intention beats beneath the surface?

This case begins on the sea — not with sailors renegotiating wages, but with a ship carrying **sugar** to Basra.

The shipowner deviated from the agreed route. The cargo arrived **nine days late**. During those nine days, the sugar market price fell. The buyer sued for the difference.

The Pulse here is the tension between:

- **Ordinary commercial risks**, and
- **Losses that are foreseeable enough to be compensable**

The heartbeat is sharper than in *Hadley* — because this is a commercial contract where both parties understand the market.

Veins — How does offer and acceptance flow?

The Veins of this case carry the flow of commercial expectation:

- The shipowner agreed to carry sugar to Basra
- The buyer expected timely delivery
- The shipowner deviated from the route
- The delay caused a foreseeable market loss
- The question becomes: **Was the price drop within the reasonable contemplation of the parties?**

The bloodstream of contract formation is flowing through **commercial awareness**.

Muscle — What gives this agreement enforceable strength?

Here is the key insight:

In commercial contracts, parties are taken to know the ordinary market risks associated with delay.

The Muscle is strong because:

- Sugar is a commodity with a fluctuating market price
- Both parties were commercial actors
- A delay naturally exposes the buyer to market shifts
- The loss was not extraordinary or unusual

This is not a special loss — it is a **market-linked, foreseeable loss**.

Heart — What is the core dispute?

The Heart of the case is the question:

Is a fall in market price during a foreseeable delay recoverable as damages?

If yes → contract foreseeability is broader than tort foreseeability.
If no → the buyer bears the market risk alone.

Spine — What rule holds this case upright?

The House of Lords sharpened the foreseeability test:

In contract, a loss is recoverable if it was "not unlikely" to result from the breach.

This is stricter than tort's "reasonably foreseeable" standard.

This Spine is the backbone of modern contract remoteness.

Brain — How does the court reason through this?

The court's reasoning is precise, commercial, and doctrinally rich:

1. Sugar is a commodity with a known, fluctuating market.
2. A delay in delivery makes a price drop **not unlikely**.
3. The shipowner should have contemplated this risk.
4. The loss was not extraordinary or unusual.
5. Therefore, the loss was within the scope of contract foreseeability.
6. Contract foreseeability is narrower than tort — but still includes ordinary market losses.

The Brain teaches students that **contract foreseeability is calibrated to commercial expectation**.

Lungs — How does this doctrine expand or contract?

This case expands contract law by:

- Clarifying the "not unlikely" standard
- Distinguishing contract from tort foreseeability
- Recognizing ordinary market losses as recoverable
- Strengthening commercial predictability

It contracts the idea that **contract foreseeability is identical to tort foreseeability**.

Stomach — The digestible takeaway

Students should walk away knowing:

- Contract damages require a **"not unlikely"** level of foreseeability.
- Ordinary market losses are recoverable.
- Commercial context matters.
- *The Heron II* refines and sharpens the *Hadley* test.

This case teaches the precision of contract remedies.

Skin — The holding

The court held that:

- A fall in sugar prices during a foreseeable delay was **not unlikely**.
- The loss was within the reasonable contemplation of the parties.
- Therefore, the buyer could recover the market loss.

Fractures — Cracks, tensions, and doctrinal shifts

- It highlights the tension between contract and tort foreseeability.
- It raises questions about how predictable markets must be.
- It contrasts with *Victoria Laundry*'s treatment of extraordinary losses.
- It foreshadows modern debates about assumption of responsibility.
- It shows the law's commitment to commercial fairness.

The fractures make the doctrine richer — because markets are unpredictable.

Case 24 — *Jarvis v. Swan Tours Ltd* (1973)

Pulse — What intention beats beneath the surface?

This case begins with something deeply human: a man who wanted a holiday that would lift his spirits.

Jarvis booked a ski holiday based on Swan Tours' brochure, which promised:

- A lively house party
- Swiss hospitality
- Yodelers
- Afternoon tea
- Fun, companionship, and entertainment

But when he arrived, the holiday was a ghost of its description:

- No lively party
- No yodelers
- No entertainment
- Barely any guests
- A lonely, disappointing experience

The Pulse here is the emotional truth:

He didn't just lose money — he lost the joy he was promised.

Veins — How does offer and acceptance flow?

The Veins of this case carry the flow of expectation:

- Swan Tours made specific promises in their brochure
- Jarvis relied on those promises
- He paid for the holiday
- The holiday delivered was nothing like what was advertised

The bloodstream of contract formation is flowing with **expectation**, not just transaction.

Muscle — What gives this agreement enforceable strength?

Here is the key insight:

****When a contract's purpose is enjoyment, relaxation, or pleasure,**

damages can include compensation for disappointment and distress.**

The Muscle is strong because:

- The very purpose of the contract was **enjoyment**
- The breach destroyed that purpose
- Jarvis suffered more than financial loss — he suffered **loss of amenity**

This is where contract law recognizes the value of human experience.

Heart — What is the core dispute?

The Heart of the case is the question:

Can a plaintiff recover damages for disappointment and loss of enjoyment when a holiday fails to match its promises?

If yes → contract law protects emotional expectations in certain contexts. If no → only financial losses matter.

Spine — What rule holds this case upright?

The court articulated a humane and modern rule:

****Where a contract is for pleasure, relaxation, or peace of mind,**

damages may include compensation for distress and disappointment.**

This Spine expands the scope of recoverable damages.

Brain — How does the court reason through this?

The court's reasoning is empathetic and grounded in the purpose of the contract:

1. The holiday was sold as an experience, not just a service.
2. The brochure created clear expectations.
3. Jarvis relied on those promises.
4. The holiday failed in almost every respect.
5. The loss was not merely financial — it was emotional.
6. Damages should reflect the **loss of enjoyment**.

The Brain teaches students that **contract law can protect emotional interests when they are central to the bargain**.

Lungs — How does this doctrine expand or contract?

This case expands contract law by:

- Recognizing non-pecuniary damages
- Protecting consumers in holiday and leisure contracts
- Acknowledging emotional loss as a legitimate harm
- Encouraging truthful advertising

It contracts the idea that **contract damages are purely economic**.

Stomach — The digestible takeaway

Students should walk away knowing:

- When a contract's purpose is enjoyment, damages can include **disappointment**.
- Misleading brochures can create enforceable expectations.
- *Jarvis v. Swan Tours* is the foundation of non-pecuniary damages in consumer contracts.

This case teaches the humanity of contract law.

Skin — The holding

The court held that:

- Swan Tours breached the contract by failing to deliver the promised experience.
- Jarvis was entitled to damages for **disappointment, distress, and loss of enjoyment**.
- His damages were increased to reflect the emotional harm.

Fractures — Cracks, tensions, and doctrinal shifts

- It raises questions about the limits of emotional damages.
- It contrasts with cases where emotional loss is not recoverable.
- It foreshadows modern consumer protection law.
- It highlights the importance of accurate marketing.
- It shows the law's willingness to value human experience.

The fractures make the doctrine richer — because disappointment is real.

10. Cost of Cure, Diminution in Value & Loss of Amenity

Case 25 — *Ruxley Electronics and Construction Ltd v. Forsyth (1996)*

Pulse — What intention beats beneath the surface?

This case begins with a swimming pool — not a factory, not a ship, not a commercial contract. A man wanted a pool built to a specific depth: 7 feet 6 inches.

The builders delivered a pool that was 6 feet deep.

It was still safe. Still functional. Still enjoyable.

But it wasn't what he asked for.

The Pulse here is the tension between literal performance and practical satisfaction. What does it mean to truly compensate someone when the breach is real, but the loss is… complicated?

Veins — How does offer and acceptance flow?

The Veins of this case carry the flow of expectation:

- Forsyth contracted for a deeper pool
- Ruxley built a shallower one
- The pool worked perfectly well
- The cost to rebuild it to the correct depth was enormous
- The difference in market value was zero

The bloodstream of contract formation is flowing — but the question is how to measure the loss.

Muscle — What gives this agreement enforceable strength?

Here is the key insight:

Damages aim to protect the promisee's expectation — but only to the extent that is reasonable.

The Muscle of the claim is nuanced:

- Cost of cure was disproportionate
- Diminution in value was zero
- But Forsyth still suffered a loss of amenity — the loss of getting exactly what he contracted for

This is where the law recognizes subjective value.

Heart — What is the core dispute?

The Heart of the case is the question:

How should damages be measured when the breach affects enjoyment, not market value?

If cost of cure is awarded → the builder pays an enormous sum for a trivial deviation. If diminution in value is awarded → the plaintiff gets nothing. If loss of amenity is recognized → the law compensates the real, lived loss.

Spine — What rule holds this case upright?

The House of Lords articulated a modern, flexible rule:

Where cost of cure is unreasonable and diminution in value is zero,

damages may be awarded for loss of amenity.**

This Spine is the backbone of modern construction and consumer damages.

Brain — How does the court reason through this?

The court's reasoning is elegant and humane:

1. The pool was safe and usable.
2. Rebuilding it would be economically wasteful.
3. The market value was unchanged.
4. But Forsyth did not receive what he contracted for.
5. The law must recognize the non-economic loss.
6. A modest award for loss of amenity is appropriate.

The Brain teaches students that damages are about fairness, not formulas.

Lungs — How does this doctrine expand or contract?

This case expands contract law by:

- Recognizing loss of amenity as a legitimate head of damages
- Allowing compensation for subjective, experiential loss
- Balancing economic efficiency with personal expectation
- Preventing wasteful awards while still honoring the bargain

It contracts the idea that damages must always be measured in market terms.

Stomach — The digestible takeaway

Students should walk away knowing:

- Cost of cure is awarded only when reasonable.
- Diminution in value may be zero even when a breach exists.
- Loss of amenity fills the gap when neither measure works.
- *Ruxley* is the modern, flexible approach to construction damages.

This case teaches the subtlety of expectation damages.

Skin — The holding

The court held that:

- Cost of cure was disproportionate.
- Diminution in value was zero.
- Forsyth suffered a real loss of amenity.
- He was entitled to a moderate award (£2,500).

Fractures — Cracks, tensions, and doctrinal shifts

- It raises questions about subjective vs. objective value.
- It contrasts with cases where cost of cure *is* awarded (e.g., defective pipes).
- It foreshadows modern debates about "efficient breach."
- It shows the law's willingness to balance fairness and economic logic.
- It highlights the evolution from rigid formulas to nuanced remedies.

The fractures make the doctrine richer — because loss is not always financial.

Part IV. Mistake

11. Objective Agreement & Unilateral Mistake

Case 26 — *Smith v. Hughes* (1871)

Pulse — What intention beats beneath the surface?

This case begins with oats — but it's really about **intention** and **appearance**.

A farmer (Smith) offered to sell oats to a racehorse trainer (Hughes). Hughes believed he was buying **old oats** (suitable for racehorses). Smith delivered **new oats** (cheaper, less suitable). Hughes refused to pay.

But here's the Pulse:

Smith never said the oats were old. Hughes assumed it.

The heartbeat of this case is the shift from **subjective intention** to **objective appearance**.

Veins — How does offer and acceptance flow?

The Veins of this case carry the flow of outward communication:

- Smith offered oats at a price
- Hughes accepted
- Hughes *believed* they were old oats
- Smith never made that representation
- The question becomes: **Does a mistaken belief void a contract when the other party never caused it?**

The bloodstream of contract formation is flowing through **objective signals**, not private assumptions.

Muscle — What gives this agreement enforceable strength?

Here is the key insight:

A contract is formed based on what a reasonable person would understand from the parties' words and conduct — not their hidden intentions.

The Muscle is strong because:

- Smith's conduct objectively indicated a sale of oats
- Hughes's subjective belief was never communicated
- There was no misrepresentation
- There was no shared mistake

This is the foundation of the **objective test**.

Heart — What is the core dispute?

The Heart of the case is the question:

Does a unilateral mistake about quality void a contract when the seller did nothing to cause it?

If yes → subjective intention rules. If no → objective appearance rules.

Spine — What rule holds this case upright?

The court articulated the classic rule:

****If a reasonable person would think the parties agreed,**

a contract exists — regardless of undisclosed intentions.**

This Spine becomes the backbone of modern contract formation.

Brain — How does the court reason through this?

The court's reasoning is crisp and doctrinally foundational:

1. Hughes assumed the oats were old.
2. Smith never said they were old.
3. Smith did not know of Hughes's mistake.
4. A reasonable person would think a contract for oats was formed.
5. Therefore, the contract is binding.
6. Subjective mistake does not void an objectively valid agreement.

The Brain teaches students that **contracts are built on outward expression, not inner thought**.

Lungs — How does this doctrine expand or contract?

This case expands contract law by:

- Establishing the objective test
- Protecting reliance on outward conduct
- Preventing parties from escaping contracts based on private assumptions

It contracts the idea that **secret intention matters**.

Stomach — The digestible takeaway

Students should walk away knowing:

- Contract formation is **objective**, not subjective.

- A unilateral mistake does not void a contract unless induced.
- *Smith v. Hughes* is the cornerstone of the objective test.

This case teaches the discipline of looking at **what was said and done**, not what was silently hoped for.

Skin — The holding

The court held that:

- Hughes's belief was subjective and uncommunicated
- Smith made no misrepresentation
- A reasonable person would think a contract was formed
- Therefore, the contract was **binding**

Fractures — Cracks, tensions, and doctrinal shifts

- It raises questions about fairness when one party knows of the other's mistake
- It foreshadows *Hartog v. Colin & Shields*, where "snapping up" a known mistake voids the contract
- It highlights the tension between autonomy and objectivity
- It shows the law's commitment to certainty in commercial dealings

The fractures make the doctrine richer — because intention is complicated.

Case 27 — *Hartog v. Colin & Shields* (1939)

Pulse — What intention beats beneath the surface?

This case begins with a sale of hare skins — a routine commercial transaction. But beneath the surface lies a pricing error that changes everything.

Colin & Shields intended to sell hare skins **per piece**. By mistake, they wrote the price **per pound** — a much lower figure. Hartog, the buyer, immediately accepted the offer.

But here's the Pulse:

Everyone in the trade knew hare skins were always sold per piece. Hartog knew the price was a mistake.

The heartbeat of this case is the tension between **objective appearance** and **known error**.

Veins — How does offer and acceptance flow?

The Veins of this case carry the flow of commercial expectation:

- The sellers made an offer with a pricing mistake
- The buyer accepted instantly
- The buyer knew the offer was too good to be true
- The question becomes: **Can acceptance create a contract when the offeree knows the offer is mistaken?**

The bloodstream of contract formation is flowing — but contaminated by knowledge of error.

Muscle — What gives this agreement enforceable strength?

Here is the key insight:

There is no contract when the offeree knows, or ought to know, that the offer contains a mistake.

The Muscle collapses because:

- The mistake was obvious in the trade
- The buyer knew the sellers intended a different price
- Acceptance was not acceptance of the *real* offer

This is the fairness limit on the objective test.

Heart — What is the core dispute?

The Heart of the case is the question:

Is a contract formed when the offeree "snaps up" an offer they know is mistaken?

If yes → contract law rewards opportunism. If no → contract law protects genuine agreement.

Spine — What rule holds this case upright?

The court articulated the fairness rule:

****A party cannot accept an offer that they know was not intended.**

There is no contract where the offeree knows of the offeror's mistake.**

This Spine prevents exploitation.

Brain — How does the court reason through this?

The court's reasoning is crisp and principled:

1. Hare skins are always sold per piece.
2. The sellers mistakenly priced them per pound.
3. The buyer knew this was a mistake.
4. Acceptance of a known mistake is not true acceptance.
5. There was no consensus ad idem — no meeting of the minds.
6. Therefore, no contract existed.

The Brain teaches students that **objectivity has limits — fairness matters**.

Lungs — How does this doctrine expand or contract?

This case expands contract law by:

- Recognizing the doctrine of unilateral mistake known to the other party
- Preventing opportunistic acceptance
- Protecting genuine agreement

It contracts the idea that **objective appearance always governs**.

Stomach — The digestible takeaway

Students should walk away knowing:

- You cannot accept an offer you know is mistaken.
- The objective test does not protect opportunism.
- *Hartog* is the fairness limit on *Smith v. Hughes.*

This case teaches the moral boundary of contract formation.

Skin — The holding

The court held that:

- The buyer knew the price was a mistake
- Acceptance was invalid
- No contract was formed

Fractures — Cracks, tensions, and doctrinal shifts

- It raises questions about what counts as "obvious" knowledge
- It contrasts with *Smith v. Hughes*, where the mistake was private
- It foreshadows modern doctrines of mistake and mispricing
- It highlights the law's commitment to preventing exploitation

The fractures make the doctrine richer — because fairness is subtle.

12. Common Mistake

Case 28 — *Couturier v. Hastie* (1856)

Pulse — What intention beats beneath the surface?

This case begins with a cargo of corn — or rather, the *belief* in a cargo of corn.

A seller contracted to sell corn that was supposedly in transit. Both parties believed the corn existed. Both believed it was on the ship. Both believed it was on its way to market.

But the truth?

The corn had **already spoiled**, had **already been sold off**, and **no longer existed** at the time of the contract.

The Pulse here is the tension between **shared belief** and **objective reality**.

Veins — How does offer and acceptance flow?

The Veins of this case carry the flow of mutual assumption:

- Seller and buyer both believed the corn existed
- They entered into a contract for its sale
- Unknown to both, the corn had perished
- The question becomes: **Can you sell something that does not exist?**

The bloodstream of contract formation is flowing — but the subject matter has evaporated.

Muscle — What gives this agreement enforceable strength?

Here is the key insight:

A contract for the sale of goods requires that the goods exist at the time of the contract.

The Muscle collapses because:

- The subject matter had ceased to exist
- Performance was impossible from the start
- There was no consideration — nothing to transfer
- The contract lacked a fundamental factual basis

This is the essence of **common mistake**.

Heart — What is the core dispute?

The Heart of the case is the question:

Is a buyer obligated to pay for goods that did not exist at the time of the contract?

If yes → the buyer pays for nothing. If no → the contract is void.

Spine — What rule holds this case upright?

The court articulated the foundational rule:

A contract is void if, at the time of agreement, the subject matter has already perished or ceased to exist, and both parties were unaware.

This Spine becomes the backbone of the doctrine of **common mistake as to existence**.

Brain — How does the court reason through this?

The court's reasoning is clean, logical, and deeply intuitive:

1. The contract was for specific goods — the corn on the ship.
2. Those goods did not exist at the time of contracting.
3. Both parties were mistaken about this essential fact.
4. A contract cannot operate on non-existent subject matter.
5. Therefore, the buyer was not obligated to pay.
6. The contract was void.

The Brain teaches students that **agreement requires something to agree about**.

Lungs — How does this doctrine expand or contract?

This case expands contract law by:

- Establishing the doctrine of common mistake as to existence
- Protecting parties from paying for nothing
- Clarifying that mutual error about essential facts voids the contract

It contracts the idea that **contracts always bind regardless of mistake**.

Stomach — The digestible takeaway

Students should walk away knowing:

- A contract is void if the subject matter does not exist at the time of agreement.

- This is a **common mistake** — both parties share the same false assumption.
- *Couturier v. Hastie* is the foundation of the doctrine of mistake as to existence.

This case teaches the fragility of agreement when reality collapses.

Skin — The holding

The court held that:

- The corn had ceased to exist
- The contract was based on a false shared assumption
- The buyer was not required to pay
- The contract was **void**

Fractures — Cracks, tensions, and doctrinal shifts

- It raises questions about risk allocation in sales contracts
- It contrasts with later cases where mistake does *not* void the contract
- It foreshadows *Bell v. Lever Bros* and the narrowing of common mistake
- It highlights the tension between fairness and certainty
- It shows the law's early willingness to void contracts for fundamental error

The fractures make the doctrine richer — because reality is not always what parties believe.

Case 29 — *Bell v. Lever Bros* (1932)

Pulse — What intention beats beneath the surface?

This case begins with corporate restructuring.

Lever Bros wanted to dismiss two executives (Bell and Snelling). To avoid litigation and disruption, they negotiated **generous compensation packages** to buy out their contracts.

After paying the compensation, Lever Bros discovered something explosive:

Bell and Snelling had previously committed serious breaches of duty. If Lever Bros had known, they could have dismissed them **without compensation**.

Lever Bros sued to recover the money, arguing:

"We paid under a **common mistake** — we thought they were innocent employees."

The Pulse here is the tension between **shared assumptions** and **the true nature of the bargain**.

Veins — How does offer and acceptance flow?

The Veins of this case carry the flow of mutual belief:

- Both parties believed the executives had clean employment histories
- Lever Bros paid compensation based on that belief
- The belief was false

- The question becomes: **Does a shared mistake about a party's wrongdoing void a contract?**

The bloodstream of contract formation is flowing through **assumptions about value,** not existence.

Muscle — What gives this agreement enforceable strength?

Here is the key insight:

A common mistake only voids a contract if the mistake makes the subject matter essentially different from what it was believed to be.

The Muscle of Lever Bros' claim collapses because:

- The executives still provided the service of "leaving quietly"
- The compensation agreement still achieved its purpose
- The mistake did not change the *identity* of the subject matter
- It only affected the *quality* or *value* of the deal

This is the modern narrowing of common mistake.

Heart — What is the core dispute?

The Heart of the case is the question:

Does a shared mistake about a party's past misconduct make a severance agreement void?

If yes → many settlements become unstable. If no → the law protects finality and certainty.

Spine — What rule holds this case upright?

The House of Lords articulated the modern rule:

A common mistake only voids a contract if the mistake is fundamental —

so fundamental that the subject matter is essentially different from what the parties believed.

This Spine becomes the backbone of modern mistake doctrine.

Brain — How does the court reason through this?

The court's reasoning is precise and conservative:

1. The contract was for severance — to end employment peacefully.
2. That purpose was fully achieved.
3. The executives' past misconduct did not change the *identity* of the bargain.
4. Lever Bros got exactly what they contracted for: termination without dispute.
5. The mistake affected the *value*, not the *nature*, of the contract.
6. Therefore, the contract was valid.

The Brain teaches students that **mistake must go to the root of the contract — not merely its desirability**.

Lungs — How does this doctrine expand or contract?

This case contracts mistake doctrine by:

- Narrowing the scope of common mistake

- Protecting finality in commercial settlements
- Distinguishing between mistakes of **quality** and mistakes of **identity**
- Making void contracts rare

It expands clarity by setting a high threshold for voidness.

Stomach — The digestible takeaway

Students should walk away knowing:

- A common mistake only voids a contract if it is **fundamental.**
- Mistakes about quality, value, or assumptions do **not** void a contract.
- *Bell v. Lever Bros* is the modern narrowing of common mistake.

This case teaches the discipline of distinguishing **essential difference** from **imperfect knowledge**.

Skin — The holding

The court held that:

- The mistake did not make the subject matter essentially different
- The severance agreement was valid
- Lever Bros could not recover the compensation
- The contract was **not void for mistake**

Fractures — Cracks, tensions, and doctrinal shifts

- It feels harsh: Lever Bros paid for something they didn't need to
- It contrasts sharply with *Couturier v. Hastie*
- It foreshadows the even stricter approach in *Great Peace*
- It raises questions about fairness vs. certainty
- It shows the law's preference for stability in commercial agreements

The fractures make the doctrine richer — because mistake is subtle.

Case 30 — *Great Peace Shipping Ltd v. Tsavliris Salvage (International) Ltd* (2002)

Pulse — What intention beats beneath the surface?

This case begins with a maritime emergency.

A ship (the *Cape Providence*) was in distress. Tsavliris, a salvage company, urgently needed a nearby vessel to assist. They contacted Great Peace Shipping, believing the *Great Peace* was **35 miles away**.

In reality, the *Great Peace* was **410 miles away** — still reachable, but not nearly as close as believed.

Tsavliris cancelled the contract and refused to pay. They argued **common mistake**: both parties believed the ships were close.

The Pulse here is the tension between **shared error** and **commercial practicality**.

Veins — How does offer and acceptance flow?

The Veins of this case carry the flow of mutual assumption:

- Both parties believed the *Great Peace* was nearby
- They entered into a salvage support contract
- The distance was much greater than assumed
- The question becomes: **Does a mistake about distance make the contract void?**

The bloodstream of contract formation is flowing — but the factual assumption is flawed.

Muscle — What gives this agreement enforceable strength?

Here is the key insight:

A common mistake only voids a contract if the mistake renders performance impossible or the subject matter essentially different.

The Muscle of Tsavliris's claim collapses because:

- The *Great Peace* could still perform the service
- The mistake affected convenience, not possibility
- The subject matter (a rescue vessel) was unchanged
- The contract still made commercial sense

This is the modern, strict approach.

Heart — What is the core dispute?

The Heart of the case is the question:

Does a shared mistake about the distance between ships void a salvage contract?

If yes → mistake doctrine becomes broad and flexible. If no → mistake doctrine remains narrow and predictable.

Spine — What rule holds this case upright?

The Court of Appeal articulated the definitive modern rule:

A common mistake only voids a contract if the mistake makes performance impossible or the subject matter essentially different from what was believed.

Mere inconvenience, increased expense, or reduced benefit is not enough.

This Spine replaces the old "equitable mistake" doctrine.

Brain — How does the court reason through this?

The court's reasoning is structured, commercial, and decisive:

1. The *Great Peace* was farther away than believed.
2. But it could still reach the distressed vessel.
3. Performance was not impossible.
4. The nature of the service was unchanged.
5. The mistake did not make the contract fundamentally different.
6. Therefore, the contract was valid.
7. The court abolished the old "equitable mistake" doctrine from *Solle v. Butcher*.

The Brain teaches students that **mistake must be fundamental — not merely inconvenient**.

Lungs — How does this doctrine expand or contract?

This case contracts mistake doctrine by:

- Abolishing the flexible "equitable mistake" doctrine
- Reaffirming the strict *Bell v. Lever Bros* test
- Making void contracts extremely rare
- Prioritizing commercial certainty

It expands clarity by giving a single, unified test.

Stomach — The digestible takeaway

Students should walk away knowing:

- A common mistake only voids a contract if it is **fundamental**.
- Mistakes about distance, cost, or convenience do **not** void a contract.
- *Great Peace* abolishes "equitable mistake" and cements the strict test.

This case teaches the modern boundaries of mistake.

Skin — The holding

The court held that:

- The mistake was not fundamental
- The contract was valid
- Tsavliris could not escape liability
- The doctrine of "equitable mistake" was abolished

Fractures — Cracks, tensions, and doctrinal shifts

- It feels harsh: the mistake was real, but not "fundamental"
- It contrasts with earlier, more flexible cases
- It raises questions about fairness vs. certainty
- It shows the law's shift toward predictability in commercial contracts
- It marks the end of dual mistake doctrines (common law vs. equity)

The fractures make the doctrine richer — because mistake is a delicate balance.

GLOSSARY OF CORE DOCTRINES

Acceptance

A final, unqualified expression of assent to the terms of an offer, judged objectively by words or conduct.

Consideration

The price of a promise — something of value exchanged between parties to make a contract enforceable.

Common Mistake

A shared, fundamental misunderstanding about a fact essential to the contract, rendering the agreement void only if the mistake makes the subject matter essentially different.

Damages

A monetary award intended to place the injured party in the position they would have been in had the contract been performed.

Diminution in Value

A measure of damages based on the difference between the value of what was promised and what was delivered.

Fraudulent Misrepresentation

A false statement made knowingly, without belief in its truth, or recklessly as to its truth.

Intention to Create Legal Relations

The requirement that parties intend their agreement to be legally binding, assessed objectively.

Invitation to Treat

An invitation for others to make offers, not an offer itself (e.g., advertisements, displays of goods).

Loss of Amenity

Compensation for the loss of enjoyment or non-pecuniary benefit when performance is defective but usable.

Misrepresentation

A false statement of fact inducing a party to enter a contract.

Negligent Misstatement

A careless statement made where a duty of care exists, causing foreseeable reliance and loss.

Offer

A clear, definite promise to be bound on specific terms, capable of acceptance.

Remoteness

The principle limiting damages to losses that were reasonably foreseeable at the time of contracting.

Rescission

An equitable remedy that unwinds a contract, restoring parties to their pre-contract positions.

Unilateral Mistake

A mistake made by one party, which may void the contract only if the other party knew or ought to have known of the error.

CASE INDEX (ALPHABETICAL)

- Merritt v. Merritt
- Partridge v. Crittenden
- Pharmaceutical Society v. Boots
- Redgrave v. Hurd
- Ruxley Electronics v. Forsyth
- Scammell v. Ouston
- Smith v. Hughes
- Storer v. Manchester City Council
- The Heron II (Koufos v. C Czarnikow Ltd)
- Victoria Laundry v. Newman Industries

ABOUT THE AUTHOR

A.G. Seymour is a visionary law tutor, compliance specialist, and author of more than twenty-four books. With an LL.M. from the University of Maryland Francis King Carey School of Law, an LL.B. (Hons.), from the University of London, and certification as a Risk & Compliance Management Professional (CRCMP), she brings a rare combination of academic rigor, regulatory insight, and creative storytelling to the study of law.

Her *Law in Pieces* series reimagines legal education through anatomically structured case dissections, bilingual clarity, and emotionally resonant pedagogy designed to spark epiphany. Anjanette G. Seymour believes that every student deserves to feel seen, capable, and at home in the law — and she writes with that mission at heart.

Beyond the page, she is a designer, mentor, and advocate for accessible legal learning, weaving art, narrative, and doctrine into a unified legacy of empowerment.

www.ingramcontent.com/pod-product-compliance
Lightning Source LLC
LaVergne TN
LVHW022222200926
848481LV00006B/2079